GROWING YOUR HERB BUSINESS

Bertha Reppert

Storey Books • Massachusetts

*The mission of Storey Publishing is to serve our customers
by publishing practical information that encourages personal independence
in harmony with the environment.*

Edited by Deborah Balmuth
Cover and text design by Meredith Maker
Text production by Wanda Harper Joyce
Cover illustration © Carolyn Bucha
Line drawings by Brigita Fuhrmann,
except for pages 8, 9, 10, 11, 12, and 13,
which are by Charles H. Joslin.
Indexed by Northwind Editorial Service

Printed in the United States by R.R. Donnelley
15   14   13   12   11   10   9   8

Library of Congress Cataloging-in-Publication Data
Reppert, Bertha, 1919–
    Growing your herb business / Bertha Reppert.
        p. cm.

    Includes bibliographical references and index.
    ISBN 0-88266-612-6
    1. Herb gardening.   2. Herbs — Marketing.   3. Herb products.   4. Herb products
        — Marketing.   5. Herb farms —United States.   I. Title.   II. Title: Herb business.
    SB351.H5R435   1994
    635.7{'}068 — dc20   93-36518
                                                                                CIP

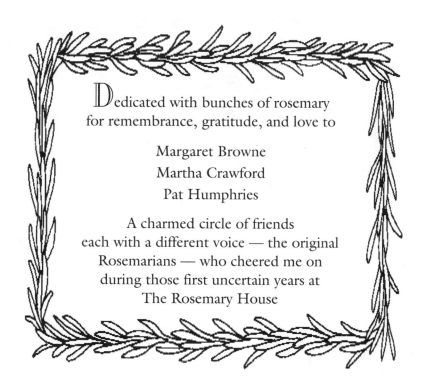

Dedicated with bunches of rosemary
for remembrance, gratitude, and love to

Margaret Browne
Martha Crawford
Pat Humphries

A charmed circle of friends
each with a different voice — the original
Rosemarians — who cheered me on
during those first uncertain years at
The Rosemary House

CONTENTS

An Herb or A Herb?

While most Americans do not pronounce
the first letter of our favorite type of
plant, Bertha Reppert always preferred
the traditional British pronunciation,
also acceptable in American English,
which sounds the 'h'. Thus, you will
find throughout this book, Bertha
refers to "a herb".

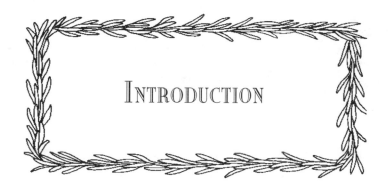

INTRODUCTION

DRIVEN FROM PARADISE, the first thing I imagine Eve saying to Adam was "Honey, dig me a little garden, just a cubit or two, so I can grow all the herbs we need close to our cave. It will be ever so handy."

We've all done that. From such humble beginnings, a new cottage industry is sweeping across America.

There are few businesses that can be initiated from a small garden — but growing and selling herbs is one. With a modest investment of time, energy, and perhaps some money, you are an entrepreneur, free to dream on into success, the pursuit of happiness, and perchance, a major enterprise.

"To begin is to be completed" is one of my many mottoes, written on a stone I use as a paperweight. Although the completion of a herb business seems never in sight, certainly beginning one can be the first giant step toward completion, starting on the day you open your doors to the public.

Beginning can be as simple as a large sign proclaiming HERBS at the entrance to your driveway. Or it could easily be a roadside stand constructed from plywood and sawhorses displaying your wares. Or you can clean out the garage, paint the walls, make frilly curtains for the windows and set up shelves, tables, and a check-out counter. As soon as you've hung your bunches of herbs, made a few wreaths, lined shelves with herb jellies, vinegars, and sugars, placed a few bins of potpourri, and flung wide the doors, PRESTO! You are in business.

What better way to celebrate our twenty-fifth year in a small herb business based on a city backyard herb garden than to share our secrets of success with others. We have learned a lot over the years and, with full confidence in our future, we encourage all so inclined to join in our pleasant pursuit. By heeding the hard-earned practical advice in this book, you can avoid pitfalls we stumbled over along our lavender-lined path.

We are proud to have spawned a host of herb businesses over the decades. Visitors from as far away as Australia seek us out on vacations and after a long happy visit to The Rosemary House take the idea of a herb cottage back to their area.

Having majored in being a Mommy, the ways of the world of business were strange to me. Terrifying too. I'll never forget our first large freight shipment when the driver poked his head in our door and demanded "Where's your siding, Lady?" I thought he was being fresh.

Now I know that the ICC regulations require truck drivers to deliver freight to a siding. No, I don't truly understand, but it's the law. Since we don't have a siding, we hire a strong neighbor boy to carry the heavy boxes off the sidewalk.

If you are in reasonably good health, have energy, stamina, and the necessary self-discipline to crack your own whip, then self-employment is a good idea. A job is always just a job but when you work for yourself you'll build a career from the ground up. To paraphrase Abraham Lincoln, if you are looking for work, start from where you are standing.

When you are self-employed, obviously the greatest plus is you are your own boss. However, it helps enormously if you can get along well with others and if you have, as I did, loyal supportive friends and family to cheer you on. I can't begin to tell you how often I enlisted their help when needed.

Other intangible assets that contribute to success are optimism, stick-to-it-iveness, and the ability to make decisions, to be reasonably well-organized, and to budget time and money. It really helps a lot to be able to sleep well at night.

The experts say poor economic times can be the best of times to start a small business and that the biggest gains in self-employment occur during slow times. However, they also point out that sixty thousand small enterprises fail every year. Perhaps that explains why the Chinese character for "disaster" is also the character for "opportunity." Ponder that.

Whether you wish to augment an income or are in need of full-time employment, the well-trod paths of a herb garden can indeed become the channel for your energies, leading to fame and fortune.

When we opened our doors twenty-five years ago, I was convinced the world was waiting with baited breath. They weren't. Opening day was our biggie that whole year. But we were happy pursuing our dream and too busy to know we weren't making any money. With herbs it's more like a calling than employment. One needs to listen to the silent voices of herbs, know their needs, and pursue their ultimate uses. But don't rush to give up your day job just yet.

We can learn much from each others' experiences. Scattered throughout these pages, I have included fifty inspiring stories of small herb businesses. (See the Appendix for a complete listing of the names and addresses of these businesses.) Since requesting these stories, my mail has soared beyond the dreary onslaught of unsolicited catalogs and contests. The harvest of heartwarming tales made trips to the mailbox worthwhile; they're a joy to read. All different, the common threads weaving through these little stories are hard work and joy, satisfaction and hope, all bound together with the love

What was Paradise,
But a garden full of vegetables
And herbs and pleasures?
Nothing there but delights.
William Lawson

of herbs. Obviously this business is not hindered by convention. Herbs provide an opportunity to start a business that fits your personality, fits your schedule, fits your budget, and fits into a spare space.

"If you build it, they will come" is another truism. Especially with the encouragement of some advance publicity. Crow about your venture. Let your friends and family and the public know about it. Send a personal note of invitation to everyone you know. Don't keep it a secret and they will come. Your new enterprise will flourish right along with your herb garden.

The one thing certain in life is change. Over the years some small herb businesses will move up — or out. Others will come along. With the exuberance of a mint plant gone wild, each business will develop a focus. But focus, too, changes over the years. To quote Henry Vaughn, "Let the herb become the teacher."

Most important, set your mind on success. If you love your work enough to persevere, and want to pursue the American dream, don't underestimate the power of herbs. Remember that time will take care of many problems and if you stick with it long enough and work hard enough, success is yours. The American dream is not an "impossible dream."

TEN STEPS TO HARVESTING PROFITS FROM YOUR HERB GARDEN

1. Plan and plant your herb garden.

2. "Let the herb become the teacher" and learn all you can while tending your garden.

3. Read, then read some more about herbs. Spend your spare time reading and learning.

4. Attend lectures, seminars, and workshops on herbs.

5. Visit every herb business and public garden within a day's radius. Include more in your vacation plans.

6. Join a herb study group. If one is not close by, invite several friends to a herb tea and organize your own group. Assign topics.

7. Subscribe to a herbal periodical or two for renewed inspiration on a regular basis. (*See* **Resources** in back.)

8. Make, use, and enjoy a variety of herbal products from your garden's harvest. Experiment with recipes endlessly.

9. Fill your house with herbs and all their by-products.

10. When you have more than you can accommodate, use, or give away, put out your sign HERBS FOR SALE.

Chapter 1

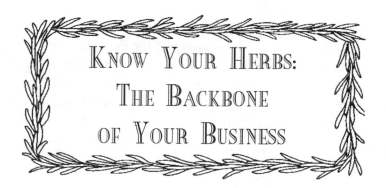

KNOW YOUR HERBS:
THE BACKBONE
OF YOUR BUSINESS

I AM ASSUMING YOU HAVE A HERB GARDEN and that you have been discovering the myriad pleasures of these eternally useful plants as you tend and harvest your garden. How else would you have learned about their generous harvest? Their endearing quiet charms? Their delightful fragrances?

Once a long while back, The Rosemary House received a letter demanding all we knew about potpourri — what it is and how to make it — because the writer was opening her herb shop in two weeks. We'll never recover from that one! Although an herb-shop owner will embrace a certain amount of on-the-job training, I strongly suggest you learn all you can well before you open to the public.

Reading provides endless amounts of good solid information. Read all you can absorb and keep reading it until you absorb more. Experimenting with herbal recipes you read about, whether it be teas, cookies, foot baths, dream pillows, or potpourri, will quickly teach you. We are fortunate. All of the herbal wisdom of the ages from all cultures and civilizations has been written down in books. Read, read, then read some more until it becomes a part of you.

In the end, the greatest inspiration to adopt herbs as a genuine lifestyle comes from the garden. "The herb becomes the teacher . . ." wrote Henry Vaughn; his words are inscribed in stone at the great Robison York herb garden at Cornell University in Ithaca, N.Y., and that's the truth.

When I first started gardening with herbs, they were hard to find. I recognized, grew, and used parsley, mint, and chives but soon my search lead me to small hidden sections of seed catalogs and obscure nurseries in search of the other herbs I was reading about. At the time, herb books were equally scarce, although that's not true today.

For instance, I learned about tarragon the hard way, by planting the seeds I felt so lucky to find. Of course, this turned out to be Russian tarragon that grew six feet tall, invaded my garden, and was tasteless. In those days of the Cold War, this was obviously a communist plot to take over; eradicating this intrepid pest became a four-year project. In the meantime I found a healthy French tarragon plant (grown only from cuttings) which quietly assumed a place in my garden and my heart, producing enough to endow gallons of tasty vinegar as well as seasonings galore, both fresh and dried. Until you taste fresh French tarragon, you cannot understand why it is the epicure's delight and why tarragon vinegar is considered top-of-the-line in demand and sales. Today every self-respecting herbal warns against growing tarragon from seed.

No one is born knowing all this. When I visited my first backyard herb garden and the gracious owner told me about thyme for courage and basil to repel flies and how to dry parsley in the oven and introduced me to all the herbal "lemons" at her disposal, it was my undoing. I knew I could never learn it all, but I wanted to.

> *HERBS — pot herbs, cordial herbs, cooling herbs, refreshing herbs — there are a dizzying number of them with names as familiar as camomile, lavender, basil, and ivy; and as unlikely as sweet gale, tonquin bean, butcher's broom, and viper's bugloss. There are dried herbs, fresh herbs, healing herbs, and cosmetic herbs. Herbs have been used throughout history in the name of love, religion, medicine, and mysticism. There are savory herbs, bitter herbs, seeds, roots, and spices.*
>
> from Mrs. C.F. Leyel,
> *Herbal Delights*

And that's true. Not a day goes by that something new, sometimes astounding, isn't introduced to my growing collection of herbal miscellany. It's natural for people, sometimes strangers, to want to share such information which I delight in writing down lest it be lost. Much of these whispered confidences is family lore.

In sum, I have learned a tremendous amount of herbal lore from reading, more from customers, and still more from my garden, the primary teacher. In a herb business, you will need every bit of information you acquire. After all, like it or not, once you open that shop door you become the expert. Customers will turn to you for answers to their questions and, as a professional who has been growing and studying herbs, you'll find most answers tucked away in your mental inventory.

Behind the front desk we have a small shelf supporting a few favorite herbals. If need be, we can always reinforce our answer with a quick reference.

Hard questions that require more research are also welcomed. We enjoy digging deeper into our large library of both the ancient mysteries and modern applications of herbs. We are glad to follow up customer questions with a phone call or note. Such continuing education is the reason we enjoy herbs so much; there's no end to the learning, all of it challenging and some of it downright amazing.

BASIC HERBS TO GROW AND KNOW: A BAKER'S DOZEN

When you consider there are ten teaching gardens at the great National Herb Garden at the Arboretum in Washington, D.C., each with one hundred and fifty herbs (that's fifteen hundred herbs) and the inventory constantly changes, a small backyard herb garden pales. At The Rosemary House we lovingly tend over a hundred different herbs, all labeled, in a downtown city garden. Not large, we consider it a teaching garden and use it frequently for individuals, workshops, or groups visiting our enterprise. In the bibliography you will find many excellent books on herb gardening and no doubt there are others. Here is a short list of our best-selling herbs, dried, fresh, in pots, or as seeds. Consider these indispensables.

1. BASIL
Ocimum basilicum
Annual; anywhere from one to three feet.
Here is an easy one to grow from seed. It germinates in three to five days, produces a fragrant seasoning indispensable to Mediterranean cookery, and is available in a wide variety of sizes, shapes, and flavors for experimentation. Besides the favorite Italian 'Sweet,' try 'Spicy Globe,' 'Licorice,' 'Lemon,' purple 'Dark Opal,' 'Anise,' 'Holy,' 'Cinnamon,' and others.

There are many more, but you get the idea. Try at least one new basil a year, grow it in full sun, and keep the flowers plucked lest it go to seed and you lose your plant. Constant pinching is the secret of long-lived bushy basils. Learn to use it in marinades, fruit salads, and tomato sauce as well as pesto. Some say it symbolizes "hate" while others claim it speaks of "love." Regardless, basil is king at the Basil Festival sponsored by Marilyn Hampstead at Fox Hill Herb Farm in Parma, Michigan.

2. BURNET
Poterium sanguisorba
Perennial; to one foot.

Available only if you grow it, burnet is a twelve-month herb. Know where you planted it and the tasty green leaves, so lovely in pressed flower pictures, can be harvested under the snow. For this reason, we always plant this herb along the path. Full sun is required and, if you allow it to flower, burnet will self-sow more plants to grow or pot and sell. It has the most wonderful flavor of cucumbers and, in fact, is called "the dyspeptic's cucumber," because it can be eaten by everyone with no embarrassing aftereffects. We love burnet vinegar (one of the best ways to preserve it) and wouldn't consider a salad without it. If you are selling fresh herbs to chefs in high hats in high places, plant lots of burnet. But don't even attempt to divide the clumps, as every plant will die. Easy from seed.

3. CHIVES
Allium schoenoprasum
Perennial; to one foot.

This is so easy and popular it hardly needs explanation. Buy a plant then divide it into four, one for each corner of a small kitchen garden. In a short while you will be able to divide these clumps again for pots of chives to sell. Everyone needs this delicately flavored onion. Seedlings can be cut and harvested when only inches high; the more you cut, the more you get. Except in May, when it blooms, we snip chives constantly. The lavender balls, gently nodding in the breeze, are welcome in the garden, in kitchen bouquets, dried for wreaths, tossed in spring salads, and absolutely breathtaking in vinegars which turn a delightful purple blush color with the delicate taste of chives captured for winter use. A best seller!

4. LAVENDER
Lavendula augustifolia
Perennial; from one foot to five feet
depending upon climate and variety.

It is my dream to sniff the fields of lavender in bloom in southern England or France. Or perhaps Tasmania in February, a good time to get away. The pictures have captured my imagination, but it is the fragrance I long to enjoy. Ahhhhhh. And yet, there are two kinds of people in the world — those of us who can't get enough of the smell of lavender and those who run gasping for fresh air when I stir the lavender potpourri. Until I tended the stand at The Rosemary House, I wasn't aware of the second group. For those who adore lavender, a gift of soaps, oils, baths, vinegar (did you know lavender is edible?), and fragrant concoctions of all sorts, tied together in a pretty basket laden with purple bows and topped with a bouquet of lavender fresh from the garden, is perfection. Grow lots of lavender — and many varieties — in the sunniest, best-drained part of your garden for fun and fragrance. It hates being grown indoors.

5. LEMON BALM
Melissa officinalis
Perennial; to three feet.

Although we wouldn't want to be without this easy-care herbal lemon, be vigilant. Keep it well clipped or you could end up with an entire garden of lemon balm. Of course, a herb business can pot up and sell all the little seedlings. It is incredibly useful — in potpourri, as tea or jelly, to repel insects (as effective as citronella), to enhance bouquets, as a seasoning and fragrance par excellence, and on and on ad infinitum. Lemon balm produces abundantly so there are no limits to the creative ways to use it. Just remember to clip your harvest. You are growing lots of profits with lemon balm.

6. LOVAGE
Levisticum officinalis
Perennial; to five feet.

I wouldn't want to live without lovage, it is a love of a herb. Because of its height, plant it where it won't shade other herbs, then keep it clipped to the desired height. Easily grown from seeds or divisions, this is another herb you will only have available if you grow it. Because it looks and smells like celery (it's sometimes called European celery), lovage is a splendid celery substitute in cookery. It is also a major ingredient in our Love Bath Balls — that's "love" as in lovage. Hung and dried in bunches, it is popular as both seasoning and decoration. The hollow stalks make great celery-flavored straws for Bloody Marys or tomato juice.

7. MARJORAM – OREGANO
Origanum majorana heracleoticum
Mostly perennial; to two feet.

The controversy over marjoram/oregano rages on. First of all, both are marjorams from the Mediterranean or Middle East. There are big lessons to be learned here, and to teach your customers and in workshops. In our area, the marjoram (*O. vulgare)* is very hardy, spreads like mint, and is a strong-flavored herb producing lovely umbels of lavender through purple flowers that dry well and are highly desirable in crafts, especially wreaths. Oreganos are the delicious pizza seasonings brought back from Greece and Italy by American GIs after World War II. Oregano, experts say, is a flavor not a species. I buy that theory because we get many plants from growers marked marjoram or oregano interchangeably. On the other hand, we have had Greek customers contemptuously spurn the same little plants with 'that's not oregano!' The true oregano requires the sharp drainage of rocky hillsides where the sun beats down on plants growing wild in thin soil, which is why it is at home on Aegean shores. The Greek oregano has compact growth, small grayed-green leaves, and a WOW! aroma that has your nose twitching and mouth salivating. Give all marjorams/oreganos the pinch test. When you come upon the real thing, you will know it. Hover over these plants, protect and nourish them, then from Zone 5 north take them into the house or greenhouse for the winter. Propagate your precious oregano by cuttings, then sell it in small bunches at a good price.

8. MINT
Mentha spp.
Perennial; variable heights.

What can I say? There are so many mints, and everyone has grown at least one at sometime or another. Don't overlook mint in your business because it is common. It's also the most popular. Propagate all your surplus into small pots and I guarantee you will sell every bit of it. We control the mints in our garden by growing them in six half-barrels. They have been transformed from invasive garden pest to a decorative feature. Who would want to live without mint? This is the one we can use to start our garden talks. Whether Brownies or senior citizens, everyone can relate to mint. Those who know nothing about herbs, and fear their ignorance will be exposed, immediately relax when mint sprigs are passed around. Grow as many kinds of mint — spearmint, peppermint, silver, curly, pineapple, apple, variegated, black-stemmed — as you have room for. They are best propagated by cutting and division; seeds are unreliable.

9. PARSLEY
Petroselinum crispum
Biennial; to one foot.

Known to everyone as the ubiquitous garnish, parsley is loaded with vitamins and minerals and should be eaten. The chlorophyll content cleanses the palate. Besides, it's reputed to "promote lust." So eat your garnish! Traditionally the seeds are planted on Good Friday and can take as long as three weeks to germinate. Plant both decorative curly and tasty flat-leaved varieties. It will be your best seller simply because everyone knows parsley. Dry it in your microwave for best color and flavor. Dried thus, in bunches, it makes a perfect Christmas decoration when combined with braided garlic, red chili peppers, and a perky bow. Remember: parsley cannot be air dried. It loses its color and that means it also loses all flavor.

10. ROSEMARY
Rosemarinus officinalis
Tender perennial to six feet.

When we agonized over a name for our herbal enterprise, we knew in the end it had to be rosemary. One of the oldest recorded herbs, it is also one of the most useful — for cooking, medicines, cosmetics, insecticides, and fragrances. Symbol of remembrance and sacred to friendship, the herb of marriage and burial, and the subject of many oft-used quotations down through the ages — it HAD to be The Rosemary House. Since rosemary is not partial to our harsh winters, we built a small greenhouse to provide winter living quarters for large old tubbed specimens that anchor our gardens during the summer. Easily propagated by cuttings or seeds, rosemary topiaries have taken the world by storm. Teach your customers that those adorable rosemary topiaries shown in many magazines perish when displayed in the center of a table. They demand light. Tend your rosemaries assiduously because you will be asked more questions about growing rosemary, especially wintering it indoors, than any other herb. Because they perish, you can count on selling every rosemary plant you have available all year round. In California, they say it's a weed.

11. SAGE
Salvia spp.
Perennial; dwarf — to one foot;
officinalis — to three feet.

There are so many beautiful, colorful sages it will be hard to choose one. Emblem of good health and domestic tranquility, sage is one of the longest lived herbs in our garden. On the other hand, it is difficult to grow indoors. Don't attempt it without grow lights. The large pebbled gray leaves bless our turkey and grace our nosegays equally well. In June we have our first generous harvest. Hung in bunches or mounted on wreath frames to dry, sage is both decorative and useful. Speak to any old-timer and sage is the herb that pops to mind when talking herbs. My Aunt Bertha went to her grave with jet black hair thanks to the sage dye bath she boiled in an old iron skillet. I tried her trick and, by Jove, it also cleans the skillet.

12. TARRAGON
Artemisia dracunculus
Perennial; to three feet.

Be absolutely sure you plant the true French tarragon that doesn't set seeds but is readily propagated from stem or root cuttings. Caution: *Don't plant anything labeled "tarragon seeds."* Your harvest, several a year, is to be guarded zealously. Treat it like the extraordinary seasoning it is. Some we dry carefully by hanging in a reasonably dark, dry place. Keep leaves whole (not crushed into a jar) so flavor is released only when crushed into special dishes. Much of our crop is preserved in vinegar, the best way to capture tarragon's unique flavor for use all year long. But nothing can beat fresh tarragon, gathered from the garden for immediate use, from early spring through late fall. You can realize a fine profit supplying fresh French tarragon to discerning chefs in fine restaurants.

13. THYME
Thymus spp.
Perennial; from one-inch creepers
to one-foot culinary types.

While "never enough thyme" may be true of your schedule, it doesn't apply to your garden. There are so many
varieties of thyme, one could have an entire garden just of
it. An ancient medicinal herb, oil of thyme still works effectively in many well-known over-the-counter cough remedies.
A favorite of bees (and fairies!), a substitute for lawn on gravelly soil, and useful for pressed crafts, teeny tiny thyme symbolizes courage. Little wonder that during the Crusades ladies embroidered sprigs of thyme on their knight's sleeves.

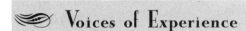 **Voices of Experience**

SHADY SIDE HERBS
AMY HINMAN-SHADE

At age ten, growing up in Ohio, Amy Hinman-Shade began learning the herb business from the ground up by helping in three different shops and gardens. Each owner had her own method of propagation, harvesting, and design, which gave Amy a broad base from which to develop her own ways.

By the time she entered college she was creating and selling wreaths for extra spending money — in a college dorm! She strung a chain by her bed to dry fresh gatherings, and when she set up shop on a sheet in the corner of her room, Amy's friends admired and willingly bought her wares.

A job at an inn took Amy to Montana, where she contin-
ued wholesaling wreaths to a local florist. Now Amy and her husband, Ron, have established Shady Side Herbs on fourteen

and a half acres five miles from Glacier National Park. They are landscaping with herbs, have extended the season with a greenhouse, and are constructing native rock raised-bed herb gardens by filling them with truckloads of topsoil. Between the thin soil (she calls it "pathetic") and the short growing season, almost insurmountable challenges face this dedicated herbalist. Because of the short season (sometimes as compact as two months) Amy plans to double her growing space and quadruple her basil production from five hundred to two thousand plants to keep up with demand.

Determined to live a herbal lifestyle, Amy looks forward to sharing her completed gardens with the over two million visitors who journey to Glacier Park each year.

HILL COUNTRY WREATHS
SUSAN WITTIG ALBERT

Like any good murder mystery, Susan's herb business has a surprising twist. Alongside the beautiful wreaths she produces, Susan writes books. She and her husband have written many children's books, and Susan herself has launched a series of herbal mysteries, beginning with *Thyme of Death*. China Bayles, her fictional heroine and counterpart, has left behind a successful career as a lawyer to open a herb shop in a small Texas town, echoing Susan's own journey. While teaching English at a Texas university, and studying the ancient goddess traditions in the "Wise Woman" ways, Susan became so captivated by herbs that she started studying and growing them.

A course in wreath-making set her off on her new career track. Using her gas-guzzling RV "Amazing Grace" as a workshop, Hill Country Wreaths was born.

Susan balances the businesses of herb crafting and writing quite nicely writing in the early part of the day, and turning to the creative therapy of

> *This book gives some slight picture of the entertainment and pleasure, the anxiety and risk, the beauty and even poignancy that lies behind our apparently quiet preoccupation with culinary, medicinal and aromatic plants.*
> Margaret Brownlow,
> *The Delights of Herb Growing*

wreath making to finish the day. Her upcoming herbal mysteries include *Witches' Bane,* about the deadly aconite, and *Hangman's Root,* an archaic name for catnip. Liberally sprinkled with herbal lore, Susan's fast-paced books are as exciting as her wreaths.

HI-ON-A-HILL HERB FARM
RUTH S. PACHECO

At age fifty-seven, Ruth Pacheco began studying herbs. An avid gardener — living on a sixth-generation, fifty-acre farm — Ruth has gradually expanded her fields to include herbs: a herbal formal bed, kitchen garden, medicinal garden, biblical herb garden, and others. But she remembers when she couldn't tell the difference between oregano and marjoram. Now she sells plants and enjoys taking customers through her gardens. "Smell and touch," she urges, "and you will learn as I did."

As a result of her studies, Ruth is a master gardener, giving herb talks and appearing on local television segments that feature herb gardening from Hi-On-A-Hill. She finds that her gardening skills and past work experience in a greenhouse and a floral craft business adapt nicely to her herbal enterprise. "There appears to be no end to where a herbal business may take you," says Ruth.

SPOUTWOOD FARM
ROB AND LUCY WOOD

"Traditionally, herbs have a meaningful spiritual quotient," says Rob Wood, caressing a sprig of rue. "More than any other plants, herbs are reminders of humankind's connection to the earth."

The Woods, both artists and teachers with a penchant for philosophy, decided in 1986 to "make our lifestyle our living, instead of living our lifestyle around our jobs."

Having moved from Baltimore to an old Pennsylvania Dutch farmstead, they began integrating their passions for the arts, land, and people by growing, selling, and teaching about herbs. While Lucy continues teaching, Rob manages their farm full-time, supervising the gardens and activities designed to create a full-fledged center for people and plants.

The twenty-six-acre Spoutwood Farm includes a traditional four-square garden; a refurbished three-story chicken barn for drying and storing their colorful, fragrant harvests; and a large, well-stocked retail shop. A quarterly newsletter announces the over one hundred events and workshops they sponsor. Their activities range from classes on plants and gardening to work-shops on flower pressing, cooking, business planning, composting, and herbal lore to story-telling evenings and herbal suppers.

The Woods' most recent addition is Dogwood House, a herbal retreat where bed-and-breakfast guests have access to a private garden, an extensive personal library, and a well-stocked kitchenette.

Chapter 2

BEFORE OPENING YOUR DOORS: BASIC BUSINESS DECISIONS

EXAMINE YOUR BUSINESS OPTIONS

PART-TIME OR FULL-TIME? Craft fairs, storefront, or mail order? Selling to the public or to a specialized group such as restaurants, gift shops, or other herb businesses? You need to answer these questions as you begin planning your own business. Many factors will affect the business configuration you arrive at, including the intended location of your business, your financial resources and the assets you already have that you may capitalize on, your special interests and talents, and the type of partnerships and networks you have established.

There is no one way to start out in the herb business, but if I could offer one tidbit of advice it would be to start from where you are — whether it be a local flea market on Saturdays, a display in a friend's store, or, if you should be so lucky, a carefully selected storefront rented with your inheritance money. Most successful herb businesses have very humble beginnings; don't feel discouraged if your resources are limited. Let your imagination run wild with ideas and keep a running list of things to try when you have the money.

ESTIMATE YOUR START-UP COSTS

What to invest in your new herb business is a variable. You can start with out-of-pocket money or approach your banker for a small business loan.

But, unless your banker shares your enthusiasm for herbs, he or she is unlikely to be a prime source of support. Your doting grandmother might better bankroll your dream. My husband's old-fashioned attitude toward borrowing money influenced our financing — "If you can't pay cash for it, you can't afford it."

Of course if you need to pay rent, you will need a bank account and a budget. Tuck away at least a year's rent money to back up your investment, watch your cash flow vigilantly, and don't quit your other job until you are sure you don't need the regular paycheck.

Theoretically this business is based on the harvest from a herb garden, produced at little cost. Indeed, the generous harvest from even a small herb garden will fill a nice-sized sales area quite profitably. If your business is home-based, all you need is a sign proclaiming HERBS directing passersby to your sales area. It is rent and overhead that eats a little business alive.

Assuming you have a herb garden to draw upon, at left is a list of basic items you'll need for a home-based business.

Actually, how much you spend on these supplies is up to you. You can make wreath forms from wire coat hangers, proudly recycle newspapers or plastic, use masking tape as labels, take the vinegar and sugar out of the household food money, and hand-draw a few flyers which can be thumb tacked to every available public bulletin board.

We haunt yard sales for baskets and glass canisters to hold potpourri, and buy every one we find for a quarter or so. It provides an astonishing variety. Run through the dishwasher, they are good as new and ready for a second life. Recycle everything that comes your way — it's not only money-

START-UP SUPPLIES FOR A HOME-BASED BUSINESS

- ❧ Business cards (most important)
- ❧ Paint
- ❧ Curtains (recycled)
- ❧ Tables and shelves (from secondhand stores)
- ❧ Flyers for publicity
- ❧ Seed envelopes (coin envelopes work well)
- ❧ Pots, soil, growing supplies (recycled)
- ❧ Pot labels (popsicle sticks)
- ❧ Baskets for display, arrangements, and gift baskets (from yard sales)
- ❧ Jellies (herbs, sugar, and pectin)
- ❧ Vinegars (herbs, vinegars)
- ❧ Jars and bottles (recycled)
- ❧ Wreaths, frames, and ribbons
- ❧ Orris and oils for potpourri
- ❧ Bags (recycled)
- ❧ Gummed price stickers
- ❧ Sales pads, pens
- ❧ Baggies

saving, it's the environmentally correct thing to do. As you can see, start-up costs can be kept to a minimum with some inventiveness and willingness to make-do.

On the other hand, if you have been working and saving toward this dream and have the money to invest, you can start with a larger and broader inventory, adding greeting cards, herbal soaps or candles purchased for resale, mugs, teas, commercially packaged spices to go with your herbs, essential oils, and other related fragrance items to your shelves. Variety will draw customers. Of course gift boxes, bags, and pretty artist-designed labels with your name and logo are additional expenses to consider. We didn't start with all these accoutrements but added them, one by one, as cash flowed in.

It's rather a thrill to plan for, save toward, and finally achieve another milestone, such as paper bags with one's own logo. We worked toward that for several years, and framed the first one. Our longstanding customers were very aware of our giant step forward and many saved and recycled our bags. One lady, however, collected them to wallpaper her bathroom, one by one.

> *Lift up your eyes upon*
> *This day breaking for you.*
> *Give birth again*
> *To the dream.*
> Maya Angelou
> "On the Pulse of the Morning"
> Presidential Inauguration 1993

Our start-up costs were negligible: We owned the building and used the rent from an upstairs apartment to pay our mortgage and overhead. Most of what we sold we made ourselves with no employees involved. If you have enough money to start on loftier levels than we did, however, you might begin figuring as follows.

As your business grows, so will your budget. If you have some savings to direct toward this endeavor and plan to rent space, here is a list of expenses you will need to take into account.

Hypothetically, with $5,000 a month to invest in inventory, using "keystone" pricing (charging double the wholesale cost) you could anticipate potential sales of $10,000 a month. A month's costs for such a business might shape up as detailed on the following page.

If all goes well and you sell all your inventory, you will cover these costs. However, a $5,000 investment in inventory does not yield an instant $10,000 in sales. At double the cost, when you sell the first six of a dozen, the supplier is paid. The next three items, selling more slowly, pay

Inventory	$5,000
Rent (or mortgage)	500
Insurance	150
Utilities (telephone, heat, electricity)	250
Employees (four, part-time)	2,000
Packaging, postage	200
Advertising (flyers, ads, posters, printing)	500
Your salary	1,000
Savings	*400*
	$ 10,000

off overhead, rent, payroll, and the like. The last three are your profit —
that is if they don't languish on the shelves forever, get damaged or
broken, or worse, stolen. Sometimes the price will have to be reduced to
sell them. There goes any hope of profit on that purchase. Now you
understand why smart buyers are prized.

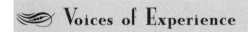 Voices of Experience

A THYME TO PLANT HERB FARM, INC.
BILL AND MARIANNE RITCHIE

The Ritchies were newly wed and operating a small, thriving catering business in their retirement when they were bitten
by the herb bug. By the time the courtyard of their condo-
minium was filled with plantings of basic culinary herbs, they
had found a five-acre farm. A cleared acre was transformed into
raised-bed herb gardens and soon they were selling a few field-
grown plants to a local nursery.

While maintaining their catering business, the Ritchies began
thinking of opening a retail herb business. The catering business
provided the income to make this dream possible. When several
garden centers inquired about buying herbs wholesale, the
Ritchies invested in a twelve- by twenty-four-foot used greenhouse. They have since added another fourteen- by forty-foot

greenhouse, a 64-foot walk-in cold frame, and a twelve-by twelve-foot potting shed to house their seeding and propagation operations.

The Ritchies' herb plants are now sold in eighteen garden centers; both Colonial Williamsburg and Agecroft Hall in Richmond purchase the Ritchies' bedding plants for their extensive display gardens.

Able to leave their catering altogether, the Ritchies have jumped into the retail arena as well. They recently were granted a variance permitting a shop on their premises, where they are selling plants and a full line of herb-related products — vinegars, seasonings, soaps, stationery — as well as a special composted growing medium and other supplies for organic herb gardeners.

> *If you would know the value of money, go and try to borrow some.*
> Ben Franklin,
> *Poor Richard's Almanac*

Heart's Ease
Sharon Lovejoy

Sharon Lovejoy, nurtured in her Grandmother Lovejoy's beloved garden of birds, flowers, and critters, felt "robbed of life" when Grandma died. She was inconsolable until she finally rediscovered her lost love of gardening in a few pots of herbs and discovered how much she enjoyed sharing herbs with others. "Even the most jaded person seems to respond to the tiniest sprig of rosemary or mint," she observed.

Sharon settled in Cambria Pines, California, a small Pacific coast town along narrow winding Highway #1, where she opened Heart's Ease, named for a favorite herb promising joy and hope, with $9 in her pocket. She felt doomed when her first customer spent only ninety-nine cents. But the magic of herbs prevailed, and customers poured off the world-famous highway all day. By her first evening she had $900 in her till.

But Sharon's trials weren't over. First, devastating mudslides hit, closing all the roads into town. Then the landlord raised the rent. She was offered another shop location by an unexpected walk-in visitor. No water, no heat, no electricity, no restrooms but the rent was cheap. She promptly moved.

Her bad luck continued — her shop was robbed! This time the community helped her out. Now working with her husband, Sharon has bought a prime piece of property, fixed up buildings, and planted gardens. A downturn in the California economy offered yet another challenge to Heart's Ease, but the company has prevailed, employing seven to nine residents and keeping a number of local cottage industries flourishing. Sharon is also a successful author, with her book *Sunflower Houses: Garden Discoveries for Children of All Ages, and more to come.*

SELECT A LOCATION

Location! Location! Location! Or so they say. This stern admonition applies to everyone except home-based herb businesses. While a site in a busy, downtown location will contribute to success, it is not essential. One thing we have learned over the years: people in search of a herbal lifestyle will seek you out. Herbs have won out over mousetraps.

We always include little herb businesses on our route when traveling at leisure — and have had adventures finding many of them. Off the numbered route, onto a one-lane road, then a left fork to a dirt lane, and finally seven-eighths of a mile opposite a numbered pole is not all that unusual. My husband, the driver, believes "out-of-the-way" is one criteria for a herb business!

There is one prominent herb farm we have visited half a dozen times, and we still manage to get lost every time. Friend husband inevitably mutters, "This one qualifies." And yet there are always other people there who have taken the trip and found it. In all cases, nice clear signs with an arrow and HERBS help the newcomer. A detailed map on every piece of literature is helpful, too.

> *It is right necessary to place Gardens near to the City, as wel for the benefit of Pot-hearbs and roots, as all manner of sweet smelling flowers, that the City greatly needeth.*
> *Were these placed in a soile far off, that they cannot so conveniently and in due time be brought to the Market to be sold, in such places they are altogether disallowed, & thought frivolous for the turne.*
> Thomas Hill, *The Gardener's Labyrinth* (1577)

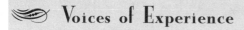

Voices of Experience

WHISKEY RUN HERB FARM
MARY SCHENCK

As a young farmer's wife and new mother, Mary Schenck dreamed of becoming a florist. She tended ever-growing flower gardens, including herbs and everlastings. By honing her floral and gardening skills, Mary turned sixty-four-acre Whiskey Run Farm into Whiskey Run *Herb* Farm.

She began in 1983, planting in a small greenhouse and an old corn crib behind the barn; by the first spring they were overflowing with flowers and herbs. A small ad in the local paper drew a host of responses from people interested in herbs and dried flowers.

Mary's husband began to take her interests seriously and moved his antiques and tools aside in the carriage house so she could set up shop. Customers demanded continued expansion, and so did Mary's gardens, eventually filling three acres. In 1990 the carriage house was enlarged to include a workroom and a classroom area. A large greenhouse was also added, joined by still another larger one in 1991. By adding classes and a newsletter, a fall open house, and a Christmas shop, Mary has transformed the historic old bootleggers' haven from a working farm with corn, hay, and cattle to a herb business encompassing her dream.

LONG CREEK HERBS
JIM LONG

Jim Long never considered opening a shop in his remote Ozarks location until his customers requested it. Up until then, he had been producing a newsletter, and conducting garden tours and workshops for garden clubs. But each group he hosted asked "where's the shop?"

At these urgings, Jim attended his first International Herb Growers and Marketers Association conference. Visiting the sales booths, seeing displays, meeting authors, and hearing recognized authorities on many aspects of the herb business,

Jim's head spun with all the new ideas. His shop plans took form on his trip home.

By borrowing $500 and scraping together $200 more, Jim began construction immediately. The money ran out before the sheetrock covered the walls, but Jim found a way and opened his sixteen- by twenty-foot shop the following year. Never mind that he is off the path, off the lane, and off the beaten road, Jim's business grew. He soon built an addition for storage and preparation, attached to the shop by a breezeway, and a second porch where guests can relax in rockers, sip herb tea, and enjoy the gardens. Over three hundred varieties of herbs flourish at Long Creek, with many producing harvest nine months of the year in this mild climate, making for a thriving fresh-herb market.

Meadow Everlastings
Sharon Challand

An article in an old *Mother Earth News* inspired Sharon Challand to plant her "field of dreams" in dried flowers. As the mother of a young son, Sharon was seeking a way to stay home while working productively. She and her husband had purchased a few acres with an old farmhouse and barn, in need of lots of tender loving care.

Her husband had a farming background and a good knowledge of field work; together they plunged into the dried flower and herb business. Sharon drew on her art background and family history (her great-grandparents ran a nursery and florist business in a small Illinois town at the turn of the century) to develop a line of wreaths, swags, arches, and flower arrangements. Growing over thirty varieties of flowers and herbs, Sharon also sells to crafts people and markets do-it-yourself kits with instructions.

Although it took several years to show a profit, the business has grown steadily. The Challands have added a small perennial nursery along with display gardens for customers to wander through. They have also launched a small mail-order service with ads in several magazines.

The Herb Barn
Nancy J. Johns

Nancy Johns was raised on a farm where she had learned to hoe — and hated it. Many years later, with her children grown and some time to spare, Nancy Johns opened The Herb Barn on a fifteen-acre farm within sight of her old homestead. A fifty-year-old barn that her father and grandfather helped raise now houses Nancy's herb shop. Surrounded by six acres planted in herbs and everlastings, Nancy is back to hoeing — and loves it. Her display gardens contain at least one of every plant they sell. They also have three greenhouses: a heated one for early propagating and overwintering tender perennials; a larger one used as a holding area between potting and sales; and a still larger one for sales.

Nancy has converted the old farmhouse into an education center for classes and workshops. It also serves as the gathering place for groups arriving for a garden tour and herb tea party.

The Herb Barn's most innovative plan is to create a school for herbal knowledge. Offered in sessions of five full Saturdays from February through May, classes will cover planning and planting a herb garden, cooking, traditional medicinals, and decorative uses of herbs. In the course of their education, each graduate will grow two hundred herb plants for their own gardens.

Along with four full-time and six part-time employees, the entire Johns family works at, supports, and encourages the burgeoning enterprise. The farm is also home to two pigmy goats, Calendula and Mugwort; two geese, Veronica and Job; and six cats, Simmy, Rosemary, Parsley, Comfrey, Tansy, and Edelweiss. The menagerie earns their keep by weeding, controlling rodents, contributing to the compost pile, and keeping children occupied while parents stroll gardens and shop.

FACTORS TO CONSIDER

If your business is in your home, your prime considerations are laws, regulations, and zoning. Our home is in a Residential I area, where in-house businesses are strictly prohibited. Make a phone call to your municipal offices to check out local zoning regulations carefully before you open. In our home, we can still tend a herb garden and have a basement workshop, as long as we sell our wares elsewhere. If you are not working out of your home, you have other factors to consider.

When we chose the location of The Rosemary House, we didn't take the admonitions about this selection seriously enough. Since we had young children, proximity to the schools was our priority. But many other important factors — parking availability, population density, proximity to other businesses, and the flow of traffic — were ignored in the process. Consequently parking at our shop is everyone's challenge, and our "off-Main Street" location makes us a bit hidden from potential customers. On the other hand, we insisted upon a shop location where we could have a backyard herb garden. No other business in town has one!

These location factors got us off to a slow start, but time and word-of-mouth have helped build our business. Indeed, we have entertained visitors from every state. And since we opened up this territory of town, several other small businesses have joined us — and we would welcome more.

At one time, Main Street would have been a better choice of location for us. We would have benefited from walk-in traffic. With the advent of several malls, our Main Street is now a vale of empty storefronts. Sadly we watch hopeful little businesses come and go because the business from dwindling number of walk-ins no longer pays the rent.

However, although a shop in a mall assures thousands of potential customers, that plus is reflected in very high rent. A full week of long hours is also mandatory in that setting, and you will need to add employees or give up working your herb garden. Your shop's focus and inventory will depend entirely upon customer demand, and you may be pulled beyond the charm and ambience of herbs you envisioned initially. Be warned — mall rents go up as your business develops.

Anyone located near a large metropolitan or tourist area has the situation entrepreneurial dreams are spun from. Seize the opportunity to cash in on the hordes of city dwellers or tourists seeking a quaint little out-of-the-way, out-of-the-ordinary tea room, herb shop, or gardens to stroll. Well publicized and stocked, your shop will not be able to contain the crowds. They will come back year after year.

The good news is that if you live on the family farm, have herb gardens to display, and roadside stands are permitted, you can hang up your sign and open tomorrow no matter where you are located. "Grow where you are planted" is good advice. A barn, building or garage makes it possible to have a larger, year-round business. Acreage leads to really big business like herb fests, craft fairs, and festivals — garlic, basil, rosemary, or faerie to name a few.

Take heart all ye who feel you live out of the way. Go nowhere without your pocket full of business cards, be sure you have a good map on it plus your hours, and let me assure you that no matter where you set up shop, in the herb business there is no such thing as an unbeaten track. Aren't you glad to hear that?

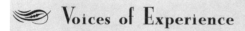 **Voices of Experience**

WILD ROSE HERBS
SUE AND JOHN THAXTER

Walking through a mall near their Texas home one day, Sue and John Thaxter came upon a group of women promoting a herb society. They didn't know thyme from marjoram, but decided to join the society and learn. They soon became hooked on herbs and took some courses in horticulture and business.

When a devastating automobile accident convinced them they wanted a different, quieter way of life, the Thaxters turned to herbs. Their search for the ideal place to establish their dream home led them to a quaint little town in southern Missouri named Hollister.

Unbeknownst to the Thaxters, while they were planting herb gardens in Hollister, the town of Branson, just four miles away, was becoming the country music capitol of the nation. Much to their amazement, the Thaxters' Wild Rose Herb Farm soon became a popular destination for vacationers seeking peace and quiet after hours of concerts and neon galore.

Soon the Thaxters transformed a cottage close to the house into a gift shop where they sell products made from the harvest of their enchanting gardens: herbal jellies, vinegars, potpourri, sachets, bath salts, and such. When visitors commented on how much they would enjoy staying close to the herb gardens, a bed-and-breakfast business was born on the farm. The Thaxters redecorated the back room of the cottage, put in a bed, and invited guests to enjoy the rockers on the porch. "Turn on the porch light to signal when you are ready for a good herbal breakfast," says Sue.

Millions of tourists visit Branson annually, while Sue and John stay in their quiet home busily adding yet another garden, waiting to share the pleasure they have found in a herbal lifestyle.

THE HERB MERCHANT
TIMOTHY L. NEWCOMER AND PAUL T. MERTEL

Begun on a shoestring in flea markets, The Herb Merchant is now a thriving business. When it became possible to purchase a building, owner Tim Newcomer paid attention to the edict on location, picking a location in the center of Carlisle, Pennsylvania, near municipal parking, neighbor to an up-scale French restaurant, in a county seat and college town. Tim opened his dream shop while continuing to work evenings at his regular job until he had built the business skills and profit margin to settle into his enterprise full-time.

From an initial line of twelve spices and fourteen herbs, The Herb Merchant now offers over three hundred varieties of herbs, spices, teas, and coffees. The shop specializes in Victoriana with potpourri and Tasha Tudor books and prints, and lures college students with incense, oils, and New Age tapes. Tim now has a partner, Paul, who is helping expand their operation to include mail order, fund-raising programs for local civic and nonprofit organizations, along with a lecture series for clubs and businesses.

Tim cautions new entrepreneurs against anticipating high profits in the early years, and warns against plunging into a high-rent district until you really know what you are doing. One of the keys to success, he advises, is to develop a specialty niche in your local area, something the mass marketers cannot underprice.

He also says: "Pursue every idea as you come up with it, without delay. If not, very soon you will read about it or see something you may have thought about doing but put off trying. Be self-motivated to act."

THE SQUIRE'S HERBARY
JUDITH MERRITT

Judith Merritt discovered success for her herb business in an unexpected place: A large mall! Judith and her photographer-husband Charles began herb gardening when they moved into a farm at the base of the Blue Mountains of Pennsylvania. Planting a few herbs seemed innocent enough, until Judith found herself constantly in search of new additions. It had become an obsession!

They planned their vacation around a International Herb Growers and Marketers Association convention and returned with enthusiasm about the potential of herbs as a business. They opened a weekend business that lured customers to their farm, did craft fairs, offered workshops, and celebrated summer and fall equinox festivals.

A story about their shop in the local newspaper increased their customer base to the point where Judith was able to quit her job and open the shop full-time. She began with herb teas and tours of the gardens, but soon realized she was spending hours teaching and entertaining visitors, while only selling a plant or two. Next, Judith began charging for her tea — entertaining her guests at elegant English high teas, using her antique linen and silver collections, tea cozies, fine loose teas, herbal pastries, hot scones, and dainty finger sandwiches. But their out-of-town location proved inconvenient for customers. Judith no longer offers teas.

And then, the break: Judith received an invitation to feature herbs at a kiosk at a large mall during the Christmas season. The rent was appalling, but she negotiated it down, with a promise of a percentage of sales — but sales were so good, she ended up paying more than the original figure! Inspired by the headiness of sweet success, Judith has moved The Squire's Herbary into a quaint house in an Allentown park.

Judith credits the distinctive business cards and labels they had designed for their vinegars and other products with contributing to their success — an expensive investment that created an impressive, successful image.

FIND YOUR NICHE: ASSESS THE COMPETITION

When starting out, you may be discouraged by the number of other herb businesses in your area — but don't despair! No two herb businesses are alike. Three herb shops in the same town may prove a surfeit, but each will no doubt exhibit entirely different philosophies, with great diversity within the specialty.

One shop may be cookery oriented with a culinary school selling seasonings, pots and pans, kitchenware and tabletop items. Perhaps a tearoom might be part of their package. Number two could be a garden shop with a greenhouse, pots of herbs available all year, sundials, and bee skeps along with outside ornaments and a herb garden planning service. The third shop might lean toward natural foods, botanicals, all sorts of herb teas, homeopathic remedies, and wonderful herbal cosmetics.

All three might well carry potpourri — the number-one top seller everywhere — and there is bound to be a certain amount of overlap. Don't worry about it. The most important thing is that you develop your own niche — your own specialties and look based on your interests and the interests of your customers.

Each shop has its own ambience…country, Victorian, modern, antiseptic, handcrafted, neat and tidy, highly organized, or higgeldy-piggeldy. Count on it, your store will have a look that is yours alone. Develop what interests you most — be it gardening, health, cooking, history and antiques, fragrance, or books — and, like an independent entity, your store will develop around that focus.

Don't waste precious time and energy worrying about the competition. Strive for success by doing the best you can, gain your customers' confidence by dealing with them fairly and earnestly, continue learning and expanding along with the new knowledge gained, and enjoy what you are doing to the utmost.

In areas where herb businesses have organized, they frequently develop a printed membership list to give to customers or post in tourist information booths. This way businesses help each other, exchanging interested customers among themselves. You will find that cooperative advertising works even better than ads for a single shop.

Our popular Traveling Herb Seminars (read "bus trips") have proven this to be true. Herb oriented, we stop only at gardens, restorations, and shops with a herb specialty. Each is invariably different. Each has its own charm, and each pulls its share of customers from our group like a powerful magnet.

Maintain your business with pride and decorum. Welcome newcomer businesses — what can you do? — and convince yourself "the more the merrier." You will soon discover that sharing the customers is sharing the wealth.

I don't know anywhere in the country where herbal businesses need to fear each other. True, competition can be threatening, but it can also be healthy, keeping you on your toes. If you join the International Herb Growers and Marketers Association (IHGMA), you automatically have all the same sources as every other member. Networking and mutual sharing can pay off handsomely. We at The Rosemary House have been asked some amazing questions about the inner workings of our business, but by answering honestly we have without fail received back even more amazing information that we can use. Be friendly . . . it comes back to you. Treat competition as an asset, a challenge that makes you better.

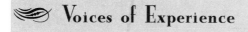 **Voices of Experience**

Penny's Garden
Penny and Don Melton

It's been a "real serendipity business," say Penny and Don Melton. Cruising along its own seemingly unguided path, Penny's Garden started as Penny and Don's Country Antiques — until they tired of traveling to shows throughout the country.

Searching for something home-based in Mountain City, Georgia, the Meltons planted a small piece of property with beautiful, colorful flowers and advertised "pick-your-own bouquets." People came, but they were more interested in buying vegetables and getting information from Penny on growing herbs than in buying fresh bouquets of flowers.

Rather than lose their lovely flowers, Penny and Don dried them — and their business underwent another metamorphosis.

They began experimenting with making herbal vinegars, and yet another product was born. They collected and recycled every attractive bottle in the neighborhood, filling them with beautiful vinegars.

People loved their rural setting, and sales were unexpectedly — and encouragingly — brisk. Penny and Don expanded their herb and flower gardens. Fired with enthusiasm, they developed a logo, designed "Penny's Garden" labels, ordered cases of new bottles, and went into full-scale, professional vinegar production.

Soon herb jellies, potpourri, sachet, and a few books were part of their line. "Mercy!" says Don, "sales tripled that year, and we were on our way to financial heights we'd never envisioned!"

Six years into the herb business and sixty years old, the Meltons thrive on working daily in their expanding gardens and visiting with their customer-friends. They have one full-time and one part-time employee, a small garden shop carrying gardening accessories and equipment, and three thousand loyal customers on their mailing list. "We are unable to imagine a greater, more satisfying life!" says Don. "Our sales are just a wonderful extra."

BACK OF THE BEYOND
SHASH GEORGI

In 1969, Shash and Bill Georgi actually lived in a tent while clearing the land for the herb gardens he designed . . . sun-dial, potpourri, free form, meditation, and culinary gardens.

Their first home on the land, the Chalet, was converted to a herbal bed and breakfast over ten years ago. Close to world-famous Niagara Falls, the bed and breakfast attracts visitors from around the world. A bottle of wine and bowl of fruit greet guests upon arrival, and Shash, a terrific cook, serves a herbal gourmet breakfast of several courses complete with edible flowers. No wonder people come back year after year.

The Georgis worked with an architect to design the main house, greenhouse, and "Herbtique," all attached to the

Chalet. Entering the Herbtique directly from the gardens and greenhouse, customers can touch, smell, or buy herb plants, gifts, vinegars, honey, peace pillows, and potpourris, along with dried flowers from the gardens.

Recently widowed, Shash plans to continue to operate the business. "The Herbtique is strictly a labor of love," she says, "...it's a twenty-four-hour-a-day hobby!"

GREEN HORIZON FARM HERB SHOP
CONSTANCE MILLER

As far as the eye can see, there is row upon row of Christmas trees at Green Horizon Farm in Bloomsburg, Pennsylvania. Her husband's tree business inspired Constance Miller to start selling herbs in their enormous barn, where her lovely shop now occupies one corner.

At Christmas, lighted trees lure customers down the lane to the farm. Of course, Constance shares the huge barn with cut trees of all sizes. Her cheerful heated herb shop offers free mulled cider, their own evergreen wreaths, and a horse and wagon ride to a site where customers can cut their own trees. Who could resist that?

Constance began with little homemade products: flavored vinegars, herb braids, and sachets. The Christmas customers expressed great interest, encouraging her to sell herb plants in the spring. From this start, she built a mailing list for classes and special events.

Now approaching thirty-five hundred readers, her three-a-year mailings announce almost weekly classes and workshops. The cooking classes held in her own kitchen fill especially quickly. Constance also conducts garden tours, which she says are a great way to sell plants faster than you can grow them.

Far out in the country, Green Horizon Farm Herb Shop relies on the tourist promotion agency to send them bus trippers. They also take the operation to street fairs, festivals, bazaars, and the popular Bloomsburg Fair, where they gain exposure to six hundred thousand people in a week.

In the beginning, the Green Horizons Farm Herb Shop was open only two days a week. Now operating Monday through Saturday, they finished their fifth year making more than they spent. Constance feels her corner of the two hundred and fifty acres "feeds the soul, gives me beauty, and keeps me in touch with God's creation."

JOIN THE HERBAL NETWORK
AND BEGIN YOUR EDUCATION

One of the best sources of business information is the International Herb Growers and Marketers Association (IHGMA). Proclaim yourself a professional by joining this association dedicated to promoting the highest level of herbal professionalism. No matter what your focus, you will find the education, services, and networking you need within this organization of like-minded people.

At the annual IHGMA conference, which takes place in a different section of the United States each year, you and other professionals have the opportunity to meet, learn, and exchange ideas. Hundreds of participants from everywhere enjoy scores of useful educational seminars, presentations, roundtables, awards, banquets, and a trade show crammed with everything your business needs.

Following the conference, you receive a copy of *Proceedings* for future reference. I find these booklets a treasure trove of useful information for a herbal business. They contain the practical experience and advice of experts. You can also buy lecture tapes to absorb at your leisure.

During the conference, the IHGMA schedules tours of successful local herbal businesses, gardens of worth, and other institutions of interest in the area. You will gain all the latest information on herb growing, propagation, arts and crafts, herbal medicine, culinary uses, promotion, public relations, packaging, labeling, FDA regulations, and on and on.

IHGMA provides an invaluable opportunity to renew and expand your network of friends and professional contacts, both nationally and worldwide. Many members are small business owners, herbal enthusiasts eager to be helpful. They share their skills and knowledge willingly. Sources of supplies, budgetary problems, computerized business problem solving, retail display and design, advertising promotions, how to enter the wholesale market, and whatever your business requires — many answers can be found through membership in IHGMA.

When you join, you receive a membership directory listing herb professionals. We herb devotees go nowhere without our handy guide to herb shops. My husband has his road atlas and I my herb business directory. It makes every vacation an outing. If, along the way, we sell some of our line at wholesale, it also makes it a potential tax deduction. It's such fun to meet our fellow herbalists, to discuss what's in and what's out, admire their crafts, sample an original seasoning, and congratulate ourselves upon choosing such a pleasant pursuit.

IHGMA also publishes an informative quarterly newsletter to keep you abreast of the latest developments and a calendar of events to help your business bloom. Of course, you can use the IHGMA logo on stationery and all your publications. It's a proud statement of unification. Since the IRS has declared IHGMA nonprofit, dues are now deductible as a related business expense. Chalk up both dues and convention expenses as "continuing education."

Write to the IHGMA national headquarters for membership information and application at: 1202 Allanson Road, Mundelein, IL 60060.

ihgma

International
Herb Growers &
Marketers Assoc.

CONTINUING EDUCATION

Much of what you do in the start-up and early operating days of your business could be classified as on-the-job-training. Having spent years as a full-time mother before starting The Rosemary House, I muddled along for awhile, learning a lot about merchandizing by trial and error. If you already have business skills, so much the better.

The more you can educate yourself early on, the better your business will be. In addition to the IHGMA annual conference, there are probably local classes and workshops to help you increase your business knowledge. In our area, the high school offers evening classes in business strategies, the local community college specializes in all sorts of business education for adults, and our state university constantly advertises short courses on entrepreneurial and managerial skills. Watch your area papers to see what courses are available to help you improve profits, increase productivity from employees, secure financing, or plan for growth.

My mail is flooded with invitations to lectures, seminars, and short courses on the business of small businesses, self-esteem, public speaking, management, government regulations, and related subjects. If this will

An Overview of Herb Businesses:
IHGMA Member Business Demographics

To better determine the type of businesses it serves, the IHGMA surveyed its member businesses in 1992. Three hundred members received the survey; over half responded, with the following result.

Age of Business: Average business is 10 years old. Half began before 1984; half after.

Form of Business: 52 percent of member businesses are sole proprietorship. 29 percent are incorporated. 19 percent are partnerships.

Retail vs. Wholesale: 59 percent retail. 39 percent wholesale. (2 percent of respondents answered "neither.")

Total Business Sales: Half of all IHGMA members have total annual sales (of all product lines) greater than $37,000 (see following table). Half have sales under $37,000. The *average* sales are about $259,000 per year ($5,000 per week).

Total Herb-Related Sales: Half of the members have herb-related sales greater than $12,000 and half have herb sales under $12,000 per year. The average herb-related sales of member businesses is $136,000 per year.

IHGMA Membership Breakdown

Total Sales	Percentage of Members	Cumulative Percentage of Members
$3,000	12%	12%
$12,000	19%	31%
$37,000	23%	54%
$60,000	6%	60%
$85,000	7%	67%
$175,000	11%	78%
$350,000	8%	86%
$750,000	6%	92%
$1,500,000	5%	97%
$3,500,000	2%	100%

give you the necessary courage to start up, by all means take a few courses. Knowledge is power, and in the world of business you can use both to your advantage.

In the beginning years, you will probably have time to devote to continuing education. Eventually one becomes caught up in all sorts of projects, new ideas, and customer demands. Even when time is getting away from you, an occasional refresher course covering pertinent small business information will be to your benefit. I'm considering the one I just read about on "how to juggle multiple priorities and meet deadlines"!

Consider joining your local chamber of commerce and other business organizations. As a member of the Pennsylvania Chamber of Business and Industry and the Small Business Services Association, I receive pertinent advice in the mail along with invitations to attend meetings, buy publications, and join in lobbying against regulations. These services are designed for the survival of small employers lost in the jungle of labor laws and taxation. Chamber membership also entitles us to many in-state tourism benefits and listings.

I find that subscribing to several herbal newsletters meets my need for current up-to-the-minute information on regulations as well as herbal developments (*see* **Resources** in Appendices). I consider marketing suggestions, growing advice, and lists of new supplier sources all part of my continuing education.

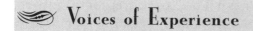 **Voices of Experience**

Quality Of Life Associates
Carol Corio

When she first experienced the aroma of a pure essential oil, Carol Corio was inextricably caught up by aromatherapy. Within a month, she was marketing a personal care aromatherapy product line part-time, and within a year she had resigned from her high-stress computer sales executive position. Quality of Life Associates was born!

Over the next two years, Carol read every book she could find on the subject; took classes, courses, and seminars wherever available across the country; subscribed to journals and publications; joined aromatherapy organizations and affiliated trade associations; and took three home-study courses. With a zeal that could not be quelled, Carol became immersed in aromatherapy. Now an expert in the field, she recently addressed an IHGMA national conference.

Under the Quality of Life umbrella are several lines of pure essential oils and related home and body products. Carol considers the oils as precious as gems, "the quintessential life-force of naturally aromatic plants, flowers, trees and herbs," she says. With that in mind, she has designed and markets "Precious Jewel Boxes," designed to store an individual's supply of small, essential oil bottles. She has also devised a clay diffuser product line to use the fragrant oils in the home. These have proven so popular that Carol has had to develop quantity production methods.

Carol's main thrust is teaching others what she has learned, transferring her passion for the "soul of flowers" so that others too may capture a whole new way of life, beginning with that first delightful whiff.

INFORMATION GLUT

Not too many years ago — a mere three or four decades — the scarcity of available basic information on herbs was a real challenge. Our town library had a book or two, and that was it. I had to dig deep for the answers to my questions and got many by doing just that, digging in my new herb garden.

Today I suffer from herb information overload. It's coming faster than I can absorb it. Our computerized society is dissecting, discussing, evaluating, re-evaluating, probing, analyzing, and generally overwhelming me with more herbal knowledge than I can use. Do you find this flood of information as intimidating as I do? Suddenly I must cope with thirty different rosemary cultivars — with the promise of more to come! The in-depth examination of thyme has produced a whole book to marvel at. It seems nothing remains at a standstill!

Every field of endeavor has produced its experts — and that's good. The inner workings of the herb world, a business that is confusing enough at its most simplistic level, are being explored and explained, researched in great laboratories, ad infinitum, ad nauseam. Specialists are developing their own fields, and if you are attracted to some narrowly focused corner of the herb world, now is the time to develop your expertise.

In the herb business, you will be asked many questions, some unanswerable even when you probe the depths of your reference library. In such cases I cheerfully give out the name of the expert in that area and go on about my weeding.

The newfound popularity of herbs has exploded into a profusion of esoteric information. Read and learn all you can, build on all the information you have already absorbed, develop a file system to keep the in-depth articles handy in case you need them, and continue to learn. Knowledge is the key to success in this business — or have I said that before?

Be not dismayed by the current information overload but rather assume that we who study herbs may well be the ones who eventually unlock some of the greatest secrets of the universe.

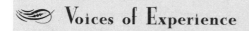 Voices of Experience

ENGLAND'S HERB FARM
YVONNE ENGLAND

Yvonne began herb gardening out of necessity. When she moved to Honey Brook, Pennsylvania, twenty-two years ago, she loved to cook French food, but many of the herbs her recipes called for were unavailable. So she grew her own — first on the windowsill, then in her garden.

Although Yvonne had a degree in English literature, gardening inspired her to return to class in the School for Horticulture at the Barnes Foundation. The more she learned, the more she gardened. Just as many others who began herb gardening as a hobby, Yvonne was inspired to start a part-time business, which expanded into a full-time one within several years.

Lectures, workshops, teaching adult education classes at several colleges as well as at prestigious Longwood Gardens, and writing fill Yvonne's time, although she has somehow also managed to develop two acres of show gardens that have been featured in many magazines. Now well-established, Yvonne's gardens feature a series of three borders with many perennial herbs, a casual four-square area, a crescent-shaped bed, a pond, a natural bog and waterside plantings. She offers garden tours by appointment for groups of fifteen or more.

The considerable harvest from all these gardens keeps Yvonne gainfully occupied fall through winter when she makes wreaths, aromatic mixtures, dried floral arrangements, vinegars, and mustards sold in her shop, The Herb Loft.

Chapter 3

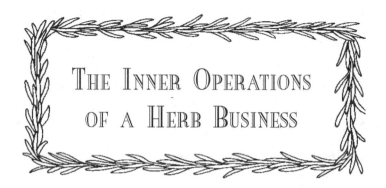

THE INNER OPERATIONS OF A HERB BUSINESS

WELL-ORGANIZED SYSTEMS AND POLICIES ARE KEY to the new herb business owner. The earlier you can decide on and set up systems, the better off you will be. This includes methods for everything from organizing financial and bookkeeping information, to ordering, inventory tracking, setting prices, and hiring staff. At The Rosemary House, we have found some tried and true systems that work well for us, as I describe in this Chapter. You may find they work for you as well, or you may want to develop new systems better suited to your individual work style. In any case, you will need to think about all these operational issues in setting up your business.

TAX MATTERS

To enter the world of business, no matter how small, most states require a resale tax number. Your state's department of revenue will issue this free upon application, along with guidelines as to what is taxable and what is not. (Look in your phone book or Yellow Pages under "Government, State" to find the Office nearest you.) From that day forward, however, you will be expected to file a tax return, accompanied by a check, on all sales. Even if you do a limited number of craft fairs during the year, you must file a state sales tax return. Don't ever assume that "no sales" equals "no return." Unless you return the form marked "no sales this quarter," the revenue department will seek you out.

For example, the Baltimore Herb Festival, a gigantic one-day event, is regularly targeted by the tax people of Maryland. Everyone exhibiting and selling is mailed a temporary tax number and tax form that must be submitted, with payment, by a specified deadline. On the other hand, a tax number allows you to buy at wholesale, to establish credit with suppliers, and to advertise your enterprise in bold print in the Sunday papers. As long as you are working alone ("self-employed"), your tax I.D. number is the same as your Social Security number. When your business shows a profit of more than $400, you will need a Schedule SE to report your own social security contributions, one more tax form to fill out, but this one is to your benefit.

If you grow large enough to require employees, full- or part-time, then you enter a more complicated tax world. You will need a federal identification number, acquired by filling out Form SS-4 at the nearest office of the Internal Revenue Service. Once you've done this you will be flooded with forms from local, state, and federal tax offices demanding immediate attention, accurate figures, and prompt remittance of all deductions such as social security, workman's compensation, health insurance, and all levies deemed essential by various government agencies either monthly, quarterly, or annually. You will need to keep very detailed records.

> *Plan your work
> then work your plan.*
> Joseph Lazur, CPA

Even a subcontractor who does $600 worth of work for you in a year must be reported. This can be someone creating all your wreaths, doing the shop stitchery, or providing your domestic help. Unless someone is an "independent contractor," reporting their own social security and so forth, the reporting burden falls on you.

Along with sales taxes, employee benefits account for a substantial amount of cash flow from our pockets to the government coffers. I am constantly amazed at how much tax money one small enterprise can generate. In order to keep up with our tax payments and stay in business, we have established a separate bank account just for withholding taxes of all sorts, including sales, income, and enough to pay our accountant. We also include money to cover building and liability insurance in this umbrella fund.

Consider also incorporating your business if you become large enough and decide to stay in the business. Incorporation can cost

$1000.00, an investment for a full-time long term enterprise. The advantages to being a corporation is that you, your equity, and all employees become a new, separate entity protected from personal liability (i.e., not subject to losing your personal assets such as your home and savings if the business should declare bankruptcy or be sued). The disadvantage is that you need a certified public accountant to figure out the tax work.

Most of this goes well beyond the garden-based small business of herbs, but you need to be aware of any government regulations that affect your enterprise, from local zoning laws to national regulatory agencies. Consult the Yellow Pages and you will discover that, in most cases, answers are just a phone call away. Failure to do so could take all the fun out of your project.

Until The Rosemary House became large enough to incorporate, the cost of merchandise plus the cost of doing business were simply subtracted from our total sales and then added to, or deducted from, our annual personal joint return. Those were the good old days. Today's complicated tax form can have one running to a tax professional for help.

ACCOUNTABILITY

As a small business owner, you have jumped into an increasingly complex world, most of it bewildering. If while struggling to survive and fighting to thrive, you can't take time out to keep abreast of ever-changing tax laws, seek out professional help, someone you trust, and let him or her answer your questions in plain English.

When we reported losses for five straight years, our accountant glared at us sternly over his glasses and said, "The IRS will look on this unfavorably as a hobby, not as a business. You are soon going to have to show a profit and pay some taxes or expect an audit." It was a rude awakening. The IRS now requires you to show a profit after three years (it was previously five years). If you don't, they want to know why.

Then he proceeded to advise us. "You must increase all your prices by 20 percent for an automatic profit." This simple bit of advice was all we needed to turn our beloved hobby into a business in the vigilant eyes of the government and send us on our way to becoming another successful small business dutifully paying Caesar his due.

BOOKKEEPING SYSTEMS

Since we do employ an accountant, I sought his advice for this section. He said in most cases, if help is required, a tax accountant will serve your needs, not necessarily a certified public accountant. At his suggestion, we use a bookkeeping system called "Ideal" which neatly charts income and expenses in one handy bright red account book. Payroll records, accounts receivable and payable, taxes paid, and all disbursements are cataloged and accessible. Available at any business supply house, this nifty system organizes the complete records you will need at the end of each year. Because of this system, we do all the book work necessary for a professional to prepare our taxes efficiently. For those inclined towards computerized operations, there is an inexpensive accounting software program called "Quicken."

TRACKING EXPENSES

Our accountant also advises that you open a separate checking account for your business and avoid paying cash for anything. Your checkbook then becomes a valuable record of expenses. If you do use cash for out-of-pocket expenses, he recommends you reimburse yourself by writing a check from the business. We do this at the end of each month, marking that check "petty cash." Substantiating receipts are kept in a special envelope along with paid bills.

Our accountant stresses that the key to what is deductible as a business expense is anything that's "ordinary and necessary," important criteria to bear in mind. I interpret this rather comprehensively: Advertising, paper wrappings, memberships in affiliated organizations, fertilizer for the garden, postage, and even the books required for my continuing education or research all qualify as "ordinary and necessary." In many ways, these essentials help support my habit — and my business.

Certainly automobile mileage is a necessary business expense. Our accountant friend strongly suggests the use of a daily logbook in which you enter mileage for deliveries, trips to the bank, or to purchase supplies, as well as excursions to present programs, lectures, or workshops. In 1993, twenty-eight cents a mile was the standard tax deduction allowed, but that could change.

If you plan to deduct your in-home office space, you cannot set up the ironing board, feed the cat, watch TV, or germinate seeds in that sacrosanct area. Since I do all that, and more, in our so-called "office," it cannot be considered dedicated and therefore it is not deductible. Deductions for home-based office space are stringently defined so check this out carefully before you file a deduction.

As you can tell, I deal with the tax collector defensively. We are quite firmly convinced that government has forgotten that small business is the real strength of this nation. "Big Brother" is not always on our side; however, no matter what it takes, I will never jeopardize in any way the delightful business I have birthed and nurtured. For as long as we want to purvey our fragrant herbs in this manner, we will keep careful records, pay whatever the law requires, virtuously hold our heads high, and continue to pursue the pleasant specialty we so passionately love.

CREDIT IS MONEY

Guard your business credit rating as if it were one of the family jewels. You can't get anywhere without it. As soon as you begin to order any type of supplies, you are going to be faced with credit applications.

When you establish credit with a supplier, they are in effect bankrolling your business with their money invested in merchandise. This generosity must be appreciated and deserves your personal attention.

In order to give you credit, most firms require some background information. Prepare a list of the following facts on your business letterhead and take copies along to gift or trade shows where you are likely to meet with suppliers:

* How long you have been doing business.
* What you sell.
* The approximate annual dollar volume of your business.
* Your state license number or federal ID number, if you have one.

Suppliers will also want to know the name, address, and phone number of your local bank and banker. Add to this the names, addresses, and phone numbers of anyone you are already doing business with so that your new creditor can check your list of credit references. They are especially interested in how promptly you pay your bills. Consistently poor marks will get you into trouble.

Because credit checks take time, a new supplier is usually willing to consider a COD (cash on delivery) shipment as a first-time convenience to you just to get the merchandise out of their warehouse and onto your shelves. For this service they may insist your first order be paid in cash or by certified check. Every business has hassled with bad checks, so this is your supplier's protection against such nastiness.

A word of caution: COD deliveries cost more because the carrier acts as a collection agency and charges an additional fee. These charges can really add up and need to be figured into the cost of doing business.

A credit card can be useful, either a personal or business account. More and more wholesalers are accepting credit cards, which save you enough in COD fees to cover the annual fee. You know, of course, that the bill is payable upon receipt of the credit card invoice, or you will be hit with a hefty finance charge. If you use your personal credit card, reimburse yourself out of the business account in order to claim the business expense deductions.

Every man is the architect of his own fortune.
Sallust

Another word of caution: Bills that are past due frequently carry a stiff interest penalty, the same as your personal credit card. Because your source is advancing you money by giving you merchandise as well as time to pay for it, this is perfectly legal. Even if you write a nice letter explaining your delayed payment, the interest continues to pile up and can be a burden.

Paying promptly will satisfy your suppliers, protect your company's good name, make others willing to extend you credit, and allow your business to grow apace. Your credit history is as valuable as money in the bank.

Getting Organized

Organization is key to your ability to handle the multiple responsibilities of a new herb business owner. A herb business owner wears many hats. She or he may already hold another paying job, working in or outside the home before donning the gardener's straw hat. Be prepared for a busy business.

A battery of file cabinets is absolutely essential to keeping organized. Suppliers' catalogs, articles you've clipped, current correspondence, and new workshop ideas can be quickly filed, and just as quickly found when needed. We keep files for everything from specific herbs — anise to

Ten Common Mistakes in a Start-up Herb Business

1. Lack of inventory. Whether you have a shop or a stand at craft fairs, you will fail without enough inventory to sustain your expenses. Purchased for resale or handmade from the herb garden, you need a large inventory. If you make it yourself, be sure to charge enough for your time and skills.

2. Uncertain hours. A locked door is uninviting. Discipline yourself to be there when you say you will be, even if you are alone making bunches of herbs to hang.

3. Inability to answer customer's questions. This is a guaranteed turn-off for customers. Although on-the-job training is acceptable, you must keep reading and learning at all times.

4. Underfunding or overextending. Watch your budget, for either way there can be deep pitfalls. If you keep track of all your expenditures, you will soon recognize financial danger spots. Monitor all of your spending and buying until cash flows in as well as out in a steady stream.

5. Slipshod recordkeeping. Well-kept records are essential for success, especially those records required by the Internal Revenue Service.

6. Inhospitality. Turn visitors into customers by welcoming them like a new best friend. After greeting them, allow for browsing. Be available but not obnoxious. Learn their names, too.

7. Poor directions. Are you hard to find? Put a map on everything and have guiding signs at every turn of the road. "If you build it, they will come" — but only if they can find you.

8. No special ambience. Create a herbal environment that attracts people and gives them something to talk about so they come back again and again, bringing their friends.

9. Going in too many directions at once. Taking on retail, wholesale, mail order, classes, lectures, crafting, gardening, luncheons, workshops, newsletter deadlines, ordering, and all the inevitable paperwork along with family, church, and community responsibilities can lead to stress and real problems in a new business, especially when you have limited help.

10. Forgetting this maxim: Start slow and grow. Above all else, stay healthy and enjoy what you are doing.

ginseng to zebrovka — to IHGMA member lists, basket sources, dried flower growers, botanical catalogs, book sources, and our stationery. A file of catalog ideas comes in handy when it's time to reprint our own.

The busier I get, the more I rely upon my bulging file cabinets filled with all I need to know for every lecture, every open house, every workshop. Here reside all our garden records, lists of workshop attendees (names, addresses, and phone numbers), menus and recipes to repeat or not to repeat, checklists of materials to assemble — whatever I need. If you don't keep all this information together, you may find yourself repeating the agony of doing each event for the first time. Well kept records become the backbone of your operation.

To help stay on track, we plan our shop's calendar of events for a full year ahead. In January we have a staff meeting to lay out all our new ideas, workshops, special luncheons, bus trips to exciting gardens — and then plunge in to schedule it all. Once it's set down, we may juggle a date or two before sending it to the printer but, by and large, dates determined in January are set for the year. It becomes the framework for our operation.

While this advance planning doesn't leave much room for flexibility, once it's done, it's done. After that you deal with it one event at a time. By March, when the little kinks have been ironed out, our calendar is off to the printer, and then mailed to our customers.

To keep myself on track, I have learned to do several things at once, just to get it all into the day. I am addicted to lists — in my purse, on the refrigerator, by the phone, and at the breakfast table. It puts everything that must be done into perspective — where I must be, what I must assemble, how to get it all done in order, and what's around the corner that I should be thinking about between priorities.

A large month-at-a-glance calendar helps control some of the work load. If there's a big herbal wedding scheduled, I know I must also set aside a block of time before the wedding date to do the harvesting, conditioning, and creative work. One of my lists includes all the supplies that need to be ordered well in advance. Another list itemizes all the bows I need to make in my spare time weeks before the wedding. You have no idea how important that single advance step can be until you are attaching all those luscious time-consuming bows at the last minute.

If I have three lectures or workshops in a row, such lists are essential, one for each event. All must be organized and set up well in advance or the stress would be unbearable and I would come unglued. Besides scheduling help in the shop and packing my props in baskets, ready to go, I must check out my wardrobe, plan family meals, take care of bills and important correspondence, water my herbs in pots, and take care of all the other daily trivia essential to keeping life going as usual.

Despite our best-laid plans, we seem only to get busier, and the need for organization becomes more important as time goes on. Sometimes things must be eliminated. For me, dropping the deadline pressure of writing a regular newspaper column was a welcome, and necessary, relief. Is there a busier business than herbs?

INVENTORY

As I've repeated many times, this is a business one can leap into with a modest investment in the bare essentials — seeds, craft supplies, business cards — but your inventory must **never** be modest.

Unless you are in a service business (weddings, catering, garden design, consulting, or producing newsletters), inventory is paramount. Whether entirely the product of garden gleanings, purchased for resale, or a mixture of both, a full and varied display of merchandise will draw customers.

I have observed that, when given many choices, your average browser will eventually find something she or he admires enough to transform them into a customer. Once the customer has actually spent time making a choice — "That one's beautiful and this one's gorgeous, but I like this one best of all" — it's a natural progression that inevitably leads to a purchase decision. I've seen it happen repeatedly.

*The best laid schemes
o' mice an' men
Gang aft a-gley.*
Robert Burns

Exciting this kind of impulse buying requires a staggering number of choices. We have inventory wall to wall, floor to ceiling, a gentle mixture of items from the garden and workshop as well as from wholesalers. But, I remember well our sparse inventory when we opened — almost entirely the work of my hands. It didn't take long to learn the reality of trying to replenish our supply of handcrafted items on a daily basis. My garden didn't grow fast enough; my schedule didn't grant enough time for all the jelly making and stitchery along with gardening. Meanwhile, our customers dwindled with the inventory.

The big difference between The Rosemary House and all the shops down on Main Street is the garden-oriented, handmade, fragrant, or flavorful herbal products we purvey. All our inventory is herbal or directly related to herbs in some way, including a mix of potpourri ingredients for do-it-yourselfers, as well as many potpourri mixtures for those not so inclined. Although we use everything our gardens produce, we have also become dependent upon other suppliers to maintain the necessary herbal inventory.

It's also important to carry items in a variety of price ranges. Along with such inexpensive staples as $2 teas, $3 mustards, $4 moth chasers, and $10 fragrant room sprays which always are sure to sell, we advise carrying upscale items such as $50 herbal prints, $100 botanical porcelains, and breathtaking wreaths at any price. One item helps sell another, and when a high-priced piece goes — which they do — we feel we can lock the doors and take a long lunch. In the meantime, these showpieces set a tone for your shop and look alluring in a window display.

Acquiring new inventory is essential. Although "trieds and trues" such as teas, candles, soaps, and notepapers are the backbone of your business, regular customers will frequently ask "what's new?" Feature a new book, a seasoning mentioned in a popular magazine, the latest garden ornament from the gift show, or a basketful of your homeworker's new tansy ant bags. We usually stage something new near the counter. Feature new items for a month or so or until it's time to showcase your next item.

TRACKING INVENTORY

Keeping track of inventory is a real challenge. Some businesses use a card file system and record every purchase and sale as it is made. You can also buy an inventory control system from an office supply store. Huge retail stores use the high-priced technology of computerized cash registers to track inventory, but anyone who has seen our burgeoning shelves would run and hide at the prospect of getting it all numbered and entered into a database.

As much as possible, our inventory is kept on the shelves. Every night we pull things forward so the shelves look well stocked, move items around to different spots where they may sell better, refill shelves, and generally aim to show off an array of merchandise. Our tracking is totally visual; we store very little in the back room, where it doesn't make any money. If the bin or shelf is getting low, we get busy stuffing our baggies or reordering from our many excellent suppliers. We call this "eyeball inventory."

Our restocking system consists of a series of reorder clipboards marked *Botanicals, Books, Miscellaneous,* and *Special Orders.* All employees are instructed to list any item on the appropriate clipboard when it is getting low or the last one is sold. After the item has been ordered, we move its listing to our *On Order* clipboard.

This quaint, old-fashioned system, devised over years of tested usage, and backed by a suppliers' file of addresses and phone numbers, works for us. Since we firmly believe in not fixing what isn't broken, our handy clipboards may well endure another quarter century. You may want to explore more sophisticated systems, available from your office supply source, or software programs if you are computerized.

PLANNING INVENTORY FLOW

Planning your inventory is an equally important task. Plan to have all necessary supplies in stock well in advance of every workshop you offer, including enough for student supplies and after-class sales. This means putting a reminder note on your calendar up to two months in advance, depending upon your suppliers and the availability of materials. We mark our supplier records "slow" or "frequently out of stock." If the supplier is "fast," we can delay ordering which usually means we order more. Our craft class supply orders are always clearly marked "In store on (month and day)." This transfers the burden of meeting the delivery date to the seller and shipper.

The Christmas season presents an inventory challenge all its own. We begin planning for the Christmas selling season with a trip to a large gift show in August, where we find a wealth of new ideas and suppliers. More and more wholesale herbal merchandise is entering the market. When we order, we stagger requested delivery dates from September 1 through November 1, with no back orders or deliveries after November 15. All our new merchandise is thus settled in before our annual Christmas Open House. We also advise our wreath makers and home-based workers to bring in their handcrafted creations before the open house. If we don't have an item on the shelves by November 15, we don't need it. Everything sells faster at Christmas.

In January, we spend a week on the arduous task of taking postholiday inventory. This is a good time to regroup what's left on the shelves and make endless lists of "wants" and "needs." Thinking of spring, Easter, and Mother's Day while we count, we are planning our future inventory as well as restocking.

This is also a good time to evaluate what isn't selling. Excess things, meaning inventory that isn't selling, represents an investment that's not producing, and costs the store money. Low turnover rates directly influence profits and, depending upon overhead, could put you out of business. Occasionally we date our price stickers to track how long merchandise is hanging around, i.e., 7/3 for July 1993. This marking is especially important for perishables that have a limited shelf life, or high-ticket items that will be reduced for sale if they don't move within a certain time period.

Because most of what herb businesses sell is related to the garden's harvest, our products have a flexibility unlike that of other shops. Fresh bunches of herbs in season are most enticing and set your enterprise apart. If they don't sell, tie on a bow, hang them to dry, up the price, and sell them later on. In the meantime, they have become part of your inventory.

We tend to order conservatively, usually just the minimum amount of an item, and then reorder if it sells well. We do this because inventory ties up money, and because we have space limitations both on our crowded shelves and in the storage area. Although many items move out quickly many times over, we aim to turn over our entire inventory at least once a year.

When ordering, be sure to take advantage of special offers such as free shipping for orders over a certain amount, free samples to serve when you introduce a new product, delayed payment (order now, don't pay for ninety days), and discounts for paying within ten days. These represent money you can use for other projects.

What to Charge?

For those of you who are "born to shop," pricing is no problem. You understand the marketplace and relative value. The rest of us need to learn about pricing our goods. It can be a hard lesson, something that takes a while. Most of us first enter this business out of love of herbs. Making a profit is not always foremost in our minds.

When you have grown choice flowers, dried them by special methods with great care, taken time to arrange them lovingly into a thing of beauty, given your work of art choice display space with all the overhead involved, perhaps had to transport it with extra care, and finally boxed and swathed it in tissues for the customer, you deserve all you can derive monetarily, whether it's done for therapy or a livelihood.

COMPETITIVE PRICING

One way to gain insight into pricing is to visit shops in a neighborhood comparable to yours, or craft fairs with artists selling goods similar to yours. This will give you an idea of what the average market price is for your goods. You can use this as a guideline in pricing your own goods, since you're not going to want yours to be much higher priced than similar goods made by your competitors.

At the same time, you want to be sure that you charge at least enough to cover your costs *and* make a profit. Figuring this amount can be a little bit trickier. You need to take into account all of the costs you're incurring. For example, even though you are growing all you purvey, don't chalk that off as "free." Fertilizers, seeds, time, and labor need to be figured in. Record the costs of all your supplies, and estimate how much is used to produce each item. Keep track of how much time it takes you to produce each item. Then figure in a minimum hourly wage for yourself, such as $10 an hour — this is part of the production costs as well. If you have employees, the wages you pay them should definitely be considered in the production costs. Moreover, you should attempt to track your indirect costs as well. expenses such as rent, utilities, show fees, travel, insurance, postage, telephone, advertising, bank fees, office supplies, packaging materials, and other miscellaneous operating costs are all part of your business' indirect costs, and should be figured into your merchandise prices. You are not going to know these costs when you first start out, but after six months or so in business, you should be able to figure out roughly how much your monthly indirect costs are. From the monthly amount, you can figure out an hourly rate for your indirect costs. This is a very useful figure to have, since you can use it to calculate indirect costs of making any particular item. For some items, you may also want to consider the cost of selling it, particularly if you do special advertising or spend hours sitting at a craft fair (compare the number of hours to how many items you sold in that period).

Calculating Indirect Costs
and Figuring Breakeven Prices

Step 1: Add up the Monthly Costs for all of your indirect expenses (i.e., all costs not figured into your direct supply and labor costs), including: rent, utilities, show fees, travel, insurance, postage, telephone, advertising, bank fees, office supplies, and any other miscellaneous costs. For seasonal expenses (such as craft show fees or travel) figure out a monthly average based on the whole year before adding in the cost.

Step 2: Monthly Indirect Costs (from step 1) ÷ number of hours your business operates monthly = Hourly Indirect Cost

Step 3: Hourly Indirect Cost x number of hours to make one of a particular item = Indirect Cost for making that item

Step 4: Indirect Cost for making item + cost of supplies + wages (and benefits) paid to self or employee for time spent making the item = Breakeven Price for item

You will also need to consider supply and demand and seasonal changes, in your price deliberations. Are you producing something that is very time-intensive *and* very popular? How many garlic braids can you produce in one season? Bear in mind, "When it's gone, it's gone" — so you must find out how much it would cost you to replace the herbs or dried flowers or garlic braids if purchased for resale from another supplier. By pricing this way, your profit may well be higher than expected on what you grow — but accept it. You deserve it.

Here's another example. If your chive blossom crop activated five gallons of beautiful, tasty, colorful vinegar, you may be tempted to sell a six-ounce bottle for $1. Don't — Mark it up to $3, or even $5. Consider that when chive blossoms are out of season, this is a fair price for a truly lovely, delicious product. If the price you set proves to be too high for your clientele and doesn't sell, it's always easy enough to reduce it.

Crafts are even trickier to price because you need to tack on added costs for creativity and skill. Take into consideration time and productivity as well and now a dollar's worth of dried flowers becomes a $40 wreath. Again be fair — fair to yourself, fair to your business, and fair to your customer. Consider the fact that there are many out there with no time or talent for crafts who greatly admire handmade items and will pay a good price for what they want. Pricing is almost impossible to move upward but reductions are an accepted practice. (There is more about pricing crafts under Co-Op Consignment, *see* page 140.)

When we have a bumper crop of sweet Annie, we can afford to sell large bunches for a dollar each. But if our harvest is limited, making it more useful to us as craft material than as merchandise, we may choose to sell it at a dollar a stem. Pricing is fraught with variables.

Most merchandise purchased for resale is marked up 50 percent. Books are usually bought at a 40 percent markup and foodstuffs at 33 percent. Unless it comes in prepriced (i.e., cards, books, and teas), we change that pricing schedule to suit ourselves. When freight costs are a significant item, we add a little bit more to everything in that shipment to absorb the cost.

All of this calculating may seem a bit overwhelming — and you may decide not to do all of it — but it does give you an appreciation for how much you're putting into the production of your wares. And chances are good that your customers will appreciate this as well.

Because we are a specialty shop, most of our customers accept the fact that overhead, attractive packaging, unusual merchandise, and various hidden costs of doing business must be included in the price. They know we are selling herbs and herb-related products they'll not find elsewhere, certainly not at the malls or outlets. This makes a difference.

When you also offer reliability, special services, personal interest, exclusivity, and unquestioned quality combined with your expertise and a guarantee, you now have a package that's unbeatable.

Don't be afraid to make a profit. You need to do that to stay in business. Think of all you can do with it! Give yourself a raise, hire helpers to free up your time, expand your domain, build a greenhouse, have a new logo designed professionally, contribute to your favorite local charity, put in another herb garden, throw an extravagant herbal festival, underwrite a program on Public Broadcasting, treat your customers to a special feature guest expert from a faraway place, have your herbal recipe collection published as a cook-booklet, ad infinitum, as long as it's tax deductible.

If your prices are out of line, the buying public will quickly let you know. In general, our one infallible guideline is this: If it sells too quickly, it is too cheap. Anything that disappears off the shelves in a matter of hours has got to be replaced at a higher price. It's called "learning the hard way." Conversely, anything that sits there and dies on your shelves needs to be repriced downward for sale. Or dusted. However, we have also observed that moving a product to another shelf sometimes gives it a new lease on life. Staging helps to sell.

Setting Hours

Tempting as it may be to close your doors and go to the movies just because you haven't seen a customer in three hours, maintaining regular business hours is absolutely essential. The day you are late in opening or, worse, don't unlock the door at all, is the day your most important customer leaves disappointed, perhaps never to return.

On snowy winter days, we listen to the school closings on the radio, then dutifully trudge through the snow to open the shop. Sometimes it's just me and the mail carrier who show up. But then there are people who like to go for walks in the snow and need to get in where it's warm and smells good. In 1972 there was a disastrous hurricane and flood named Agnes which closed our doors, as did the famous nuclear incident at Three Mile Island in 1979, when most of the area was evacuated. Except for such unpredictable disasters, we are there when we say we will be. Determining days and hours of operation and then abiding by them is a decision of utmost importance. You don't have to be open every day, but whatever your schedule, it needs to be clear for your customers. Like most shops in our town, we are closed on Mondays. We have learned to schedule our doctor's appointments, committee meetings, and visits to other herb businesses on Mondays.

There are many shops that advertise their operations as "by chance or by appointment." If you are at home to hear the clanging of your outside bell or the ringing of your phone, that's your signal to open. Some who work at other jobs choose only weekend hours. Others find mornings are the most convenient time to tend shop. Herb businesses can be flexible, especially when operated out of the home.

And then there are those for whom there is no idleness. Open seven days a week, ten hours a day, like a mall operation, this forms the framework of their lives. So be it. Actually, if the truth be known, I probably work ten hours or more on most days. Much depends on the individual business owner's lifestyle and stamina.

Many small specialty shops close after Christmas for a January vacation. Others sell out their potted plants over July and close for August. These are decisions to consider. Obviously, if you are lucky enough to be in a tourist area, you wouldn't dream of taking off during the height of the season.

Since we are running a mail-order business with customers in California, Maine, Texas, along with neighboring (less wintery) states, we must always be available to answer the phone even if *we* just got twelve inches of snow. Besides, slow days offer a good time to clean, change the front windows, catch up with paperwork . . . and fill mail orders.

HIRING STAFF

This is a not a business for everyone. You have to want to do herbs and spices. Therefore, our best employees are those who seek us out, who have been our customers, taken our classes, or obviously have fallen under the magic spell of our pleasant specialty. If they are interested in herbs — culinary, crafts, medicinal, or growing — and are seeking part-time employment that requires continuing education, we are happy to have them join our team. Especially if they are willing to work on Saturdays and during the holiday season.

The one on-the-job training we've found it necessary to offer is how to make change. Computerized cash registers have deprived an entire generation of that skill (and they can easily be cheated). A few carefully monitored trial-and-error bouts with making change teaches almost anyone quickly.

Another asset we seek in prospective employees is the ability to talk easily to customers, answer their questions, and handle several customers with speed and accuracy, while keeping everything under control. Although we treat everyone equally, we also encourage each employee to develop their special abilities and interests.

For a while we had a lady with a flowing hand who manuscripted all our shop signs. Everyone commented on our matched signage. Another employee was a wizard with weeds, making the most exquisite wreaths, which we gladly sold for her. When we were lucky enough to employ a knowledgeable herb gardener, we promptly elevated her to "Head Gardener" and had special name cards imprinted for her to use. "This is better than a raise," she told us.

We want our personnel to take our customers seriously, to listen to them, be receptive to their ideas and questions, and pass on their feedback to us. We want our staff to offer assistance without being pushy or aggressive. We encourage shoppers to enjoy our shop as much as we do by allowing people freedom to browse.

Occasional staff criticism is offered with great care, in a positive way with specific guidance for the next time. We also solicit employee suggestions for improving on every in-store operation, and involve all of them in every aspect of the business. Versatile staff members who take initiative and are flexible keep the business going day to day.

Pricing new items, rearranging or stocking shelves, stuffing baggies with bows, dusting and sweeping are everyday chores that always need attention. In summertime, watering herb plants in pots leaps to the top of the list, and we hire additional part-time help in the garden. We impress upon every employee that The Rosemary House has been built on unflagging "busy work." Seemingly endless lists are posted on handy clipboards so there is never a cry of "what's next?" We are well aware of the problem of too much to do and too little time. But we keep going, whittling away at the lists, glad to be working with fragrant herbs.

We may not always pay as much as we would like to, so we try to make up for it in other ways:

- ❀ A week's paid vacation.
- ❀ Attendance at all classes and special events free or at cost.
- ❀ Occasionally we send out for pizza and have a group luncheon and discussion period.
- ❀ When hired, they are told they are not being hired to be the janitor but they must sweep and dust occasionally and clean the commode weekly, as much a chore here as at home.
- ❀ They are trained in "suggestive selling," an easy, inexpensive way to add on sales. If someone buys orris root, we ask, "Do you need oil to go with that?"
- ❀ At the register, checking out, we ask, "Can we get you anything else today? Have you seen our new product?" (always at the counter).
- ❀ We teach the staff to reassure sales — for example, "I think that's beautiful, I've been admiring it myself" — or words to that effect.

❀ When selling at craft fairs, it pays to talk to customers. We always have samples which we tout loud and clear — "That's our best-selling seasoning, we've been making it for twenty-five years." Sitting isn't selling . . . talking makes the sale.

Always generous with our praise, we are pleased to accommodate special requests from employees and want everyone to be as happy working at The Rosemary House as we have been. We treat our working team as a family, trained to provide personal, courteous service to keep our customers coming back. This approach to staffing has been invaluble in keeping us in business.

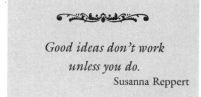

Good ideas don't work unless you do.
Susanna Reppert

Make It a Family Enterprise

There isn't a child alive who hasn't played "store." Here's their chance to step into a real skill-developing situation par excellence. Instead of fooling around, watching TV, or being bored, our children were suddenly very much needed, and they proved their worth.

Starting at an early age, twelve or so, the girls tended the store on a regular basis, alternating Saturdays so their school activities were not excluded. We worked out mutually agreeable schedules with equal hours for all. Summer vacations always included time off for camp or swimming parties but, again, work schedules built a framework to their days. Free time became a very precious commodity and still is.

They had to meet and talk to strangers, answer questions, add up lists of figures correctly, make change (without a computer), take charge in any situation, make decisions, water plants, dust, and sweep. A small family-based business is a total real-life learning experience.

Of course, they didn't know all the answers at first, but it was impressed upon them that teaching and information were vital to our success, and they were firmly instructed to get answers from me or from our reference books or take down questions and tell the customer we would get back to them. In most instances, the answer was a mere phone call away.

There were certain basic questions that popped up again and again. These they soon learned to answer with great authority. What pride they took in their new skill! With every question, their herbal knowledge developed apace.

We no longer do craft fairs because the children who loved them and helped so willingly are grown and gone. But what great family fun it was while it lasted. Eager to set up, eager to tend the stand, eager to make a big sale, they really enjoyed it more than I did. Again, we wrote out a schedule so everyone had a turn or two strolling around to enjoy the fair and time off, with money, for lunch.

The secret to such agreeable cooperation is that they were paid for their work — modest amounts, it's true, but eventually they all had bank accounts and attainable goals. And the business had another legitimate deduction to report.

Without denying themselves small pleasures, our children used their income to buy coveted clothing, to take trips abroad on Eurailpass, to buy a car, or to provide some extras for college. Being gainfully employed gave them a work ethic, a sense of values, and money in the bank. It was thrilling to watch them develop into self-assured young ladies who walked with purpose, and our little business deserves a lot of credit for this accomplishment.

This training carried over to include girlfriends and neighborhood teens who wanted to join in our fun. They may have gone along for the ride, but eventually they found themselves at work, greeting strangers, answering questions, developing poise and self-assurance along the way and pocketing a bit of money.

We still employ and train high school students for part-time positions. The first thing they learn is there are no stupid questions, and, second, there is no such thing as idle hands. Insurmountable piles of busy work are always awaiting hands to do it even while waiting patiently for indecisive customers to make their decisions. When one of our trainees left for college, she said, "I'm smart enough to know I'll never have another job as wonderful as this one."

Susanna, our youngest daughter, now manages The Rosemary House. As a grade schooler, she came to the shop every day after school and we still have her little desk where she crayoned and, later, did homework. Susie absorbed the answers to all the questions like a sponge. The day she graduated from college, she came to The Rosemary House as usual and said, "O.K. Mom, you can go home now and play with your toys. I'm taking over." So she did, and I did go home. The Rosemary House is now in the hands of a second generation. I often feel envious of these children who had the advantage of all this herbal knowledge decades before I

SUSANNA REPPERT SPEAKS

Other herbal business owners often ask me, "How do I get my children interested in my business?" I tell people not to pressure their kids into anything. I never felt pressured into work because I was always paid for my time. I might not have been allowed to cash my checks until the Christmas money came in, but I was always compensated monetarily — and in other ways too.

People thought my mother was smart to hire family she didn't have to pay. But no indeed, she paid all of us full wage — and sometimes more. She says, "If I don't pay them, I'm going to have to give them money anyway. They might as well work for it and make it a payroll deduction."

Another important thing is that I was always given freedom in my high school years to do other activities, such as debate team or the school plays. In summer I wouldn't have been allowed to watch TV anyway, but an occasional day to raft the Yellow Breeches Creek was allowed.

The other important point was that my ideas were encouraged. If I thought of a new store display or felt a certain product should be developed, it was always considered and usually worked on.

People often say, "You're so lucky to have your mother." But my mother always says, "I'm so lucky to have her." It's that sort of attitude that keeps families in business.

Most of the time family in business is a virtue, but it would be a lie to say it's always a box of chocolates. The major problem seems to be a tone of voice. With an employee, you speak softly and always say "please" or "thank you." Because you expect family to understand, you often speak in short, abrupt sentences and expect the blanks to be filled in, which can lead to hurt feelings and misunderstandings.

However, having family in your business can be the best thing. You get twice the work, twice the loyalty, twice the caring for half the money. Although family members can also be demanding, they are frequently more dependable, trustworthy, and show more initiative. These are assets money can never buy.

stumbled onto it. They have been given a great gift, far greater than the paychecks, although they may not yet realize it.

Today, as a family corporation, we look forward to our annual corporate board meetings when, all adults now, we analyze our mistakes, discuss future plans, and have a great time doing it. Afterward everyone receives a basket of new herb products from our annual crop.

ALLOWAY GARDENS AND HERB FARM
BARBARA STEELE AND MARLENE LUFRIU

The real estate agent in Littlestown, Pennsylvania told Barbara Steele, "You'll like your new neighbor. She grows the same thing you do!" Now, seeing the gardens and sales area on the Steele property and the production/greenhouse areas located next door on the Lufriu farm, one wonders what invisible hand guided this alliance.

Alloway Gardens has grown gradually, as an integral part of the lives of these two families. At first they grew plants in a nine-by eleven-foot greenhouse and cold frames, were open just a few weeks in spring, and offered a few herb classes. At shows, they passed out literature, newsletters, and information about the farm.

In the meantime, the Steele farm developed a sales area (a log house purchased and moved log by log), a lath house, a wagon shed for classes, and display gardens. At the same time, a ninety-six-foot, double-poly greenhouse and adjoining lath house was constructed on the Lufriu property. They were in business!

Now open six days a week spring through summer, weekends from fall through Christmas, and other times by appointment, the business is a grand mix of education, service, and sales. Marlene, trained as a medical technician, enjoys the greenhouse production work and keeping business records. Barbara's background is in art education. She prefers horticultural research and uses her artistic skills to design display gardens, arrange the sales area, and do advertising layouts.

The extraordinary partnership of neighbors bordering the Alloway Creek is now marching toward its second decade, growing busier all the time. As Barbara says, "We've planted a herb garden that got out of hand."

Sinking Springs Herb Farm
Ann and Bill Stubbs

Sheltered by an ancient sycamore, sprouted in 1578, the Stubbs' eighteenth-century family farmhouse and restored barn provide the perfect setting for garden tours, herbal luncheons, and herb craft and wildflower classes.

A husband and wife team with shared interests, Ann and Bill Stubbs combined their enthusiasm for dried flowers and herbs with their interests in art, history, poetry, gardening, and cooking to create a home business. When introduced to herbs and their lore, Ann says, "It was like opening a door to a new world. Once we stepped through it, there was no returning." In The Garden Cottage, the Stubbs offer private overnight accommodations and a generous country breakfast laced with herbs to travelers seeking a cozy retreat at the crest of the Chesapeake.

On appointed Thursdays and Saturdays, the Stubbses put on programs featuring herbal-icious gourmet foods, fresh and unprocessed, served in the old house. Private parties, bus tours, garden clubs, and other interested visitors keep them busy all summer serving food and conducting garden tours.

In the winter, they provide in-home demonstrations of dried flower and herb creations and offer a wedding flower preservation service. They are noted for their skill at drying and arranging special occasion bouquets under glass, and this specialty maintains their income adequately while the gardens sleep.

Ann traces her enthusiasm for herbs to her mother, who loved nature and kept their home filled with flowers. Bill is fascinated with herbal lore, which he translates into poetry, sold in slim volumes in The Mux'n Room, their seventeenth-century gift shop stocked with all their garden produce.

Ann and Bill caution that "a husband and wife business team must take constant care not to lose sight of the husband and wife relationship. A blending of business and personal relationship takes skill and constant sensitivity," they note. "But we feel our success is a testament to its ability to work."

MARI-MANN HERB CO., INC.
MARIBETH JOHNSON

Maribeth Johnson started Mari-Mann Herb Company as a hobby, selling herbal blends, seasonings, jellies, and sauces out of her kitchen (using a temporary license from the Health Department). Maribeth, the daughter of a wholesale grocer who supplied private-label products to midwestern stores, understood marketing. With the support of her husband, Bob King, a banker and public relations expert, Maribeth began transforming her hobby into a wholesale and retail business, renting land with a tumbledown cottage and planting an acre of herbs.

Bob's unexpected death pushed Maribeth deeper into her enterprise, motivated by both financial and emotional needs. Her eighty-five-year-old mother joined her, and with assistance from her sons and a daughter-in-law, their labor of love began to grow.

When a customer called to ask "how much kitchen potpourri should I use on my pot roast?" Maribeth began her famous Thursday luncheons and Cooking with Herbs School series, always filled to capacity. She offers wreath workshops, craft, and gardening classes as well.

Maribeth's sons Joel and Mike have joined her full-time in the business located in Decatur, Illinois. Mike has developed patented solid scents and is working on other Mari-Mann products. This multigenerational herb business has burgeoned from a kitchen-based hobby to a full-blown, growing family enterprise.

Chapter 4

SETTING GOALS AND
PLANNING FOR THE FUTURE

A FEW YEARS AFTER WE OPENED THE ROSEMARY HOUSE, a professor from a nearby university came calling. He was investigating small businesses and their goals. Alas, I had neglected laying down plans. Laughingly I told him my goal was "to stay alive." "That's a good goal," he conceded. Often clinging to a thin hair economically, we *have* managed to stay alive and, in reality, have strived for goal after goal, advancing in an orderly progression over more than two decades.

The professor sent me a copy of his findings: 85 percent of the small businesses that responded had plans and goals. Half of these had put their plans in writing. And, most interesting, the planners seemed to outperform the nonplanners in their businesses.

Setting goals, attacking the project, developing a workable program to make it happen involves everyone. Teamwork and determination can pay off handsomely. Although we never had a proper written plan for the total development of The Rosemary House, over the years we have indeed set and met certain goals — which, in turn helped us catch the brass ring of success. Our first dream was to have a small greenhouse. Since I'm married to a man who believes "if you can't pay for it, you can't afford it," it was exciting for me to watch the bank balance mount to meet the estimate for our greenhouse. Now twenty years old, it has fulfilled its promises, and we are studying a larger, more efficient, more expensive replacement. There is, need I say, a bank account abuilding for the purpose.

More recent goals include acquiring a computer and printer for our handouts, a portable speaker system for our bus tours and garden talks, fifty matched workshop chairs, and privacy fencing to enclose our three gardens. The first three goals have been realized, but that last one — the fencing — costs a hefty amount that will take a while to accumulate.

A new high-rise, low-maintenance garden with easy-care, eighteen-inch-high beds was another of our dreams that has come true. We enjoyed planning and saving for it — now we love to tend it. We can sit on the edges to weed! This advanced our cause while it also took care of a developing problem . . . bus tour groups arriving with increasing frequency, and we had no place to entertain them. Now we have nine new small theme gardens to talk about while the visitors sit comfortably on the sturdy frames. I never enjoyed speaking to a standing audience, and now we no longer need to. The small, powerful, portable microphone will make our garden tours even better.

Actually we have one consistent goal that has energized us since we initiated our first new product — wedding rice with roses and rosemary — way back in June 1968, a month after opening. That's when we realized our customers would seek new products among the old familiar standbys. Ever since, it has been our goal to devise something new for our shelves every single month.

Proving the eternal usefulness of herbs, each month another Rosemary House product adds interest to our inventory, luster to our wholesale list, and keeps us looking for additional ideas to develop. A product a month — or at least twelve a year — has been a challenge that has kept both our imagination and our business busy.

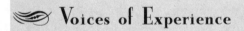 **Voices of Experience**

GREENFIELD HERB GARDEN
ARLENE AND PAT SHANNON

Starting very small in 1980, the Shannons never envisioned the phenomenal growth of their herb business. They began with a farmers' market stall; for one summer of Saturdays they sold herbs cut fresh from their garden. Their initial investment consisted of two handmade tables, Mason jars, lots of educational signage, and an umbrella for shelter.

The following year they attended the farmers' market from June through October adding herb plants, dried bunches, and crafts such as potpourri, catnip mice, and herb wreaths. In the third year, they attended craft shows and opened their house several days a year for special sales. All this went on while they held down full-time jobs and raised their family.

When the income from herbs equalled her salary as a teacher, ArLene quit her sixteen-year career where she felt "burned out and underpaid." They started looking for a permanent home for their enterprise. During a visit to pictur-esque Shippshewana, an Amish-Mennonite town in rural northern Indiana, she found it. Although they hated to leave Chicago, this was too good an opportunity to pass up. It also meant that Pat would have a one-hundred-and-fifty-mile commute for eight years until retirement in 1992.

Now their store has expanded from a small cottage to a handsome two-story barn with double the space, a greenhouse, plant house, pavilion, a floral design area, and display gardens. Here customers can select from over three hundred varieties of herb plants, over four hundred book titles, and a host of herb-related products. In summer, when Shippshewana bulges with thirty to sixty thousand tourists, it takes ten employees to keep the Greenfield Herb Garden going.

They have since moved out of the Ma and Pa apartment over the shop to a new home on thirty-four acres nearby — "in case we have dreams of expanding," explains ArLene.

HONEYSUCKLE LANE
LINDA COOK AND BARBARA GOODMAN

Honeysuckle Lane is proof that you can begin a small retail business without a bank loan, an in-depth business plan, or any marketing expertise. It's a bit tricky, but this energetic mother/daughter team have proved it can be done.

Started in a six- by eight-foot potting shed in Linda's side yard, Honeysuckle Lane now occupies a thirty- by sixty-foot renovated barn loft. Because they listened to their customers (mostly women employed outside the home like Linda and Barbara), they learned what to stock, how to give them the classes and information they need, and, more important, the best times to be open.

A seasonal operation spring and fall, they have part-time hours. They found the best time to schedule classes is Thursday evenings. However, they always stress they are only a phone call away at any time. They're available whenever a customer needs to contact them, with an answering service to ensure a quick reply.

The dynamic duo admit to making two serious errors: not subscribing to *The Business of Herbs* sooner, and waiting to join IHGMA, both major resources for the small herb business owner. They say these would have been major steps for a smoother, simpler journey.

Beginning as a shared activity based on backyard herb gardens they both enjoyed enormously, at first they offered primitive garden benches, garden plans, seeds, and a few plants.

Now they have added everything you can imagine that's herb related combined with their spring workshops ranging from garden plans and organic pest control to making herbal vinegars and skin-care products. In the fall their workshops are focused on creating dried swags, wreaths, and other herbal decorations. They often stop and ask themselves, "How did this happen?"

They made it happen through a growing mailing list, a newsletter crammed with customer lure and information, occasional appearances at craft fairs, and their own diligent continuing education by attending lectures, seminars, and workshops. They recently added a half-acre of beds to provide more herbs and flowers. Now a driving force in both their lives, "Honeysuckle Lane seems to be on a course all its own and we just run to keep up," says Linda.

Before You Start:

Guidelines for Goal Setting

Some of us set goals and achieve them without further ado. However, this takes a person with extraordinarily focused determination and single-minded purpose. Everyone else, especially those with a family, job, and other distractions, needs to jot them down.

To keep all your thoughts in one place, get yourself a nice clean three-ring notebook and a pack of paper, and start doodling away. Dividers are a nice touch. Jot down names for your enterprise, ideas for merchandise, garden plans and suppliers, "things to do," your favorite crafts, hobbies, quotes and notes for inspiration and motivation, and all your hopes, dreams, and goals. Write them down: page upon page of everything you can think of; this is your roadmap. Convoluted as it may seem, it can lead you to success.

Eventually you can sort out your doodles into proper lists. Consolidate generalities under page titles: projects, locations, what you excel at (and what you don't), herb plants you have and those you want to acquire, your heart's desires, your assets, finances available, furnishings you can use — even shopping lists count.

Now your plans are taking shape. Toss into your considerations the amount of time you can devote to your enterprise. While you are thinking about time, estimate when you could be open to the public. Include the names, addresses, phone numbers, and special skills of friends who would enjoy playing along — those who sew, who make bread, jellies, or vinegars you could sell for them; talented flower arrangers; and artists to design flyers, labels, and your business card.

Start a separate page just for your business card. List everything pertinent you can possibly squeeze onto it. See pages 96-97 for specific ideas on what to include.

Buy yourself another pack of paper and forge on. Do you want stationery, printed bags, and reams of informational handouts for your customers and students? Then you'll need to make a list of local printers, their addresses and phone numbers. Add their printing estimates to your notes if you can get them.

He started to sing
as he tackled the thing
That couldn't be done,
and he did it.
Edgar A. Guest

Do you want to have students? That means offering classes and workshops — more lists. What will you teach, where will you teach it, to whom and how many, where and how often? Morning? Noon? Or night? Write it all down. It's always easy to cross out ideas that prove unworkable later.

Now you will have to think about advertising, always important, especially for a business-to-be. You are rolling along, listing every possible source of free publicity for a limited budget. Read Chapter 5, "Marketing and Public Relations," then add all your own creative ideas for spreading the word about your business.

By all means, include a budget page. This is fraught with variables, but start somewhere (*see* pages 17 – 20).

If you plan to do craft fairs, make another section for that information. List where and when they are held and who the contact person is. Call for pricing and reservation information, then set a goal of six or eight fairs a year (or however many you feel you can stock. Remember the more inventory you *have*, the more you will sell). List your inventory possibilities along with tables, backgrounds, shades, chairs, and staging available, yours or theirs.

Certain extremely popular craft fairs may require getting on a waiting list. Do so immediately because you can always cancel if it is no longer convenient when eventually your name comes to the head of the list. Jot down essentials to pack, such as food cooler, thermos, cash box, marking pens, masking tape, plastic bags, sunhats, and so forth. I find this little checklist most helpful. Write them down.

Now you are thinking of more things to add to your preopening ideas. Organization is taking place in your mind so it's time to sort through the welter of random thoughts and restructure them into something positive and definite. Label your dividers. Fill in names, addresses, and phone numbers of appropriate people, including suppliers and any professionals you may need (banker, lawyer, accountant, county agent).

Unless you plan to sell out of your home, a page on location will be useful. List parking needs; your building requirements for storage, workspace, kitchen, restroom, and so forth; population density; other businesses in each area you are considering; traffic flow; rentals; and all other pertinent information you will need.

Goals = Projects. Perhaps you should list your projects in order of their priority, such as the following.

Week 1:   Choose the sales spot.
Plot the place on paper in your workbook.
(Design business card.)

Week 2:   Start painting and fix up.
(Make potpourri.)

Week 3:   Move in tables and shelves.
(Make sachets.)

Week 4: Assemble boxes, baskets, crates, and the old baby crib to display pillows.
(Make wreaths, garlands, and sprays for ambience and to sell.)

Week 5: Fill displays and containers listed above with merchandise.
(Make jellies and vinegars.)

Week 6: Set date for the grand opening and herb tea party.
(Plan menu.)

Week 7: Get out publicity.

LOOKING BEYOND OPENING DAY

Go beyond grand opening day to plan your year (*see* "A Year in the Herb Business," pages 105 – 109) and set goals month by month on your personal calendar. Take time to write out your plans in great detail in your workbook and they will become reality. Don't discard any idea until you have written it down and given it some thought. You'll be amazed at how an initial proposal can change into a truly remarkable, feasible inspiration just by sleeping on it. But first you need to spell it out.

Think ahead to next year and set more adventurous plans — even dare to write out where you want your business to be in five years. They say a goal without a plan remains a dream. Here's a five-year plan to consider. Use several pages and make yours more aggressive if that's your inclination. Bear in mind that the secret of getting ahead is getting started.

Year 1: Do six craft fairs. Make and sell from the herb garden. Gather names for a mailing list.

Year 2: Continue craft fairs. Design and stock a shop area in the old shed. Plant another garden next to the new shop.

Year 3: Use mailing list to advertise an open house party on May 1 to introduce the shop and gardens. Reduce craft fairs to the three best ones.

Year 4: Organize "First Sunday" herb tea parties and "Third Thursday" workshop/classes by sending out another enlarged mailing. Plant another, larger herb garden.

Year 5:   Sales have more than doubled; time to enlarge shop/ workshop area and start mail-order catalog. Go part-time on the day job. Hire some help.

Putting it down can force your fairy godmother to grant your wishes. Goals happen — if first you set them down.

Your workbook is now mushrooming beyond its boundaries, some of it built upon previous jottings. By now you are no longer a shy stranger to the task but rather an eager entrepreneur raring to jump in. If the notebook habit has taken hold, you will be adding more ideas as the old ones are scratched off.

At this precise moment, for instance, I have a list of twelve new products to develop for this year, with five already crossed off the list and on the shelves. By applying my time, energies, and thoughts to the remaining seven, some in progress, all should be accomplished by the end of this year. Moreover, we have begun our thinking and planning and twelve-new-products list for next year. To hold that thought, jot it down.

> *The first part of life should be spent developing passionate hobbies, and the second part in indulging those hobbies and keeping young and engaged with that passion.*
> Julia Childs (at 80)

When we first opened a few hours a day, five days a week, back in 1968, our goal was $20 a day or $100 for the week: A fortune! Found money from our garden and handicrafts. Since we paid no rent and those were the days when a dollar bought a dram of oil or a bottle of spice, we were quite happy with such a modest goal. Meeting it meant jubilation in the household and exciting plans to add to the inventory.

Time, expertise, mail order, inflation, and a greatly expanded inventory have changed all that. But whether you set a goal of $10 a day — or $100 — or $1000 (yes, it's possible) — write it down. Pin it to your mirror so you see it first thing every morning and you will make it happen, using all the jottings in your burgeoning notebook. Eventually, instead of a workbook doodler, you will become a very busy doer.

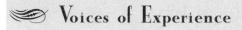

SUNSHINE HERBS
DENISE AND BRYON PROVENCHER

Denise and Bryon Provencher fell in love with each other — and with herbs — on a first date at Caprilands Herb Farm in Coventry, Connecticut over a lemon geranium. Smitten by the sweet scent of this lovely plant, they bought it, took it home, and started a herb garden at their home in Haverill, Massachusetts.

As they added plants, their love and their garden flourished. And so they were wed. Eventually, as will happen with herbs, they had too many plants. What to do? The local farmers' market became their first outlet, and was a heady success. Many customers were drawn to the market just to visit Sunshine Herbs. Soon restaurants and caterers discovered their fresh and dried products and the orders flowed in.

Although their best seller is from-the-garden potpourri blends and sachets, they also pride themselves on a large selection of organically raised herbs, potted as well as freshly cut. They also deal in dried herbs, culinary products, mixed seasonings, oils, and breads.

Catnip mice are hard to keep in stock, along with herbal moth protector bags. The Provenchers are constantly looking for changing trends and new products to add to their line.

Besides the farmers' market, Denise and Bryon also exhibit at area craft shows and horticultural events. They give talks on herbs, and particularly enjoy visiting private homes to design herb gardens.

Everything comes out of their beautiful gardens which have now grown to include a perennial border, a water garden, a raised rock bed, and a special romantic alcove. This private retreat gives them quiet moments to sniff sweet lemon geranium together all the while dreaming of bigger and better adventures with Sunshine Herbs.

WALTON'S HERBAL WARES
LINDA WALTON

Soon after Linda Walton began selling at craft shows as a hobby, her home was overflowing with herbs: a separate entrance for a shop and a large amount of growing space became the criteria for a new house in Wentzville, Missouri. Linda's shop plans are on hold as she is busy raising her two daughters and teaching full-time, but the space is ready and waiting for her after she retires.

In the meantime, Linda's gardens and knowledge grow, and her products become more professional with each passing year. She works fifteen craft shows annually, sells fresh herbs in the spring, publishes a newsletter and a mail-order catalog, teaches a junior college class on herbs, and speaks to garden clubs and other groups.

"Herbs became a part of my life in my childhood, when my mother sent me out to the herb garden to collect certain varieties for the meal she was preparing," writes Linda. Now her own children continue the tradition, helping Linda pick, sniff, and taste the herbs fresh from the garden just as Linda did.

Linda was greatly encouraged to learn at an IHGMA conference that the median age of women owning and operating herb businesses is fifty plus. That thought keeps her going as she looks forward to her fifties when she plunges into her second career — herbs full-time.

THE LAVENDER HOUSE
CAROLINE MOSS

Inspired by the stories of many small successful American herb businesses that she has read about, Caroline Moss hopes to generate a similar enthusiasm for herbs in England. A law school graduate specializing in taxation, Caroline turned to a home-based business out of a desire to be able to care for her young son.

Using her home herb garden in West Midlands, England as a base, Caroline teaches a course on herbs at the local community college. She promotes her business, The Lavender House, through a herb newsletter she publishes and press releases to local media (relying on free advertising as much as possible, out of necessity).

In addition to selling herbs through her newsletter, Caroline also enjoys operating a stall every Saturday morning at the local Woman's Institute Market. Here she test markets some of her herbal products, sells baked goods featuring herbs, and carries a line of American herb books not generally available in England. Many of the authors of these books are the source of her own inspiration.

Caroline offers the following business advice, which is worth passing on to other herb business entrepreneurs:

- Devise a relatively limited business plan and assign real dates for accomplishing each goal.
- Learn as much as possible from similar businesses.
- Be attentive to your customers; give them your time, recipes, and advice freely.
- Teach about herbs at every possible opportunity; people really want to learn.
- Start small with limited products; test market and establish good business practices before determining your precise concentration and niche in the market.
- Tend your herb garden — a must for both your sanity and continued education.
- Don't underprice your goods.
- Present a professional image.
- Maintain a strict but flexible timetable for accomplishing your business goals so that things don't get beyond your control.

BUFFALO SPRINGS HERB FARM
DON HAYNIE AND THOM HAMLIN

After twenty-four years in the florist business, Don Haynie and Tom Hamlin were looking for a change — and herbs seemed to be just the thing. They had enjoyed many inspiring visits to the world-famous Caprilands Herb Farm in Connecticut and developed a close friendship with Adelma Simmons, the owner. In 1988 they attended the IHGMA conference to explore the possibility of converting their herb hobby into a business.

The following year Don and Thom traveled throughout the Midwest visiting a variety of herb businesses and developing a vision for their own. Their florist business sold that same year, and — free at last! — they launched a search for the right spot for their herb business. The farm they chose was "the worst-looking place of all, but it had possibilities," says Don of their one-hundred-and-seventy-acre Buffalo Springs Herb Farm in the Shenandoah Valley of Virginia.

They began a huge restoration project on the eighteenth-century stone and brick house, the barn, springhouse, granary, gardens, and grounds. (The stunning transformation they accomplished was featured in the December 1992 issue of *Colonial Homes*.) They opened for business in August 1991 — but no one knew about them! They flooded the area's information centers, bed-and-breakfast inns, motels, colleges, and universities with brochures, and the business took off.

Herb programs, workshops, Sunday teas, herbal luncheons, a retail shop in their grand nineteeth-century barn, refreshments, house tours, and guest speakers, along with gardens and acres of lawn draw people from all over. With a nature trail, display gardens, and a picnic area on their grounds as well, Don and Tom are busier than ever, but agree that the rewards are worth it.

SHALE HILL FARM AND HERB GARDENS
PATRICIA K. REPPERT

In 1969 Pat Reppert considered opening a small business packaging and selling herbs — culinary, bath, and potpourri — but was stopped dead in her tracks by the Small Business Administration. They denied her a small business loan telling her she needed to find suppliers, research FDA rules and regulations, determine her marketing strategy, and "about forty other things I've now forgotten," sighs Pat.

When the Repperts moved from Manhattan to Shale Hill Farm in Saugerties, New York, Pat's husband, a cardiologist, built an office onto their home, which he intended to use as an apartment upon his retirement. As this date approached, however, Pat's plans for a herb business resurfaced. The would-be apartment is now her shop.

Before opening, Pat filled four notebooks with brainstorming ideas for her business, exploring all her interests and skills. She also drew on the resources of the IHGMA. After exploring her options, antiques and herbs won out.

Besides stocking all things herbal, Pat prides herself on offering a wide variety of fine gifts, one-of-a-kind wedding and birthday presents, and interesting items, ranging in price from fifty cents to many hundreds of dollars for some of the antiques.

She also sponsors workshops and guest speakers of note. She initiated a "Garlic Festival" that was so successful it quickly outgrew her premises and has been taken over by the local Kiwanis Club as a fund-raising project.

"The gardens are really at the heart of what I'm trying to do here," says Pat, "which is to excite people about the possibilities of herbs and how they enrich people's lives. The gardens provide pathways back through time into different cultures, bringing sense-tingling flavor and fragrance to foods, mind-lifting aromas to the environment, and a sense of connection to the earth and its life-giving bounty."

DEVELOPING A FIVE-YEAR PLAN

Time and time again, I have seen small ventures fold after three, four, even four and a half years. Nothing makes me sadder because just as frequently the fifth year is the turning point.

Underfunding, grim business setbacks, and economic realities all can pose serious, seemingly insurmountable problems. If you brace yourself for such eventualities from the beginning, know that small businesses are the most vulnerable to failure, and continue on your course no matter what, be assured that you and success will meet sometime after the fifth anniversary. It has happened again and again. Almost all businesses that survive the first uncertain five years will continue onward to success. To reach this five-year plateau, your business will need to go through a growth-and-discovery process to find a market niche and establish a customer base that will ensure a profit. This does not come easily.

You will probably find the direction of your business changing dramatically, perhaps several times over the first five years. You must listen to your inner voices, pay attention to your customers, and "let the herbs become the teacher."

Perhaps you started with an experimental roadside stand, selling surplus plants and fresh bunches. Eventually you might find yourself moving indoors and serving herb tea on the porch. Or, customer's questions may lead you into presenting impromptu little lectures. By then, you are lining the porch with shelves, filling them with all the wonders from your garden, and expanding your inventory. You quickly realize every item you mention in a talk is sold before it is returned to the shelves.

> *Let us then be up and doing,*
> *With a heart for any fate;*
> *Still achieving, still pursuing,*
> *Learn to labor, and to wait.*
> Longfellow,
> "Psalm of Life"

Budding customer interest may lead you to enlarge your gardens, initiate workshops for small groups, or contemplate adding a greenhouse. Responding to customer interests — and anticipating new ones — is critical to your success. Many enlargements and improvements take time and energy along with as much cash as you have for the step forward. Sometimes advancement is as simple as extending your hours for greater customer convenience — no money involved in that.

I can tell you that after our first five years in business, suddenly our gross income doubled. Just as suddenly, it doubled a second time the following year. For the first time we understood cash flow — the experience of having cash flow **in** faster than it flowed out — and felt like a proper business. Since our fifth year, despite inflationary spirals and economic downturns, our gross income has increased consistently, and the bottom line improves annually. Despite grim reports in the business news, we have been encouraged to carry on by the climbing interest in herbs, our enlarged inventory, and the unprecedented growth of our customer base.

Stick to your dreams as long as you possibly can. Forge onward, go for the brass ring. The first five years are not the basis on which to judge your fledgling herb business. It is merely prologue. By having a five-year plan in mind from the beginning, you will not become impatient just as you border on success. For some it will come sooner, but it's not fair to yourself or your enterprise to give it less time.

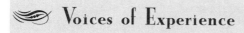

HONEY ROCK HERB FARM
DEE AND JIM BROWN

Their fifth year in the herb business proved to be the turning point for Dee and Jim Brown at Honey Rock Herb Farm in Louisville, Tennessee. That's when they recognized their main focus — plants — and knew they had a business.

Up until then, Dee and Jim had been running the gamut: growing herbs, supplying fresh-cut herbs to restaurants and markets, making herbal vinegars, jellies, and blends, traveling the craft-fair circuit with their wares, and writing an informal seasonal newsletter (their only form of advertising). Replacing a back porch with a lean-to greenhouse gave Dee and Jim more space to start plants, and to host group visits. When they sold $300 worth of plants to a visiting garden club, they realized to their amazement that they were doing something they enjoyed, *and* making a profit.

As their herb-growing enterprise grew, they discovered more people were coming to visit and buy. "Everything came together in this magical fifth year," note the Browns. They gave up the craft-show circuit, focusing their energies on plants rather than crafts.

When a friend in the wholesale plant business moved out of state, Jim and Dee bought her small hoop greenhouse and started contacting her list of wholesale garden customers. Now they are knee-deep in seedlings, soil, and fish emulsion and love it, measuring their success by Henry David Thoreau's adage (in box).

> *If the day and night are such that you greet them with joy, and life emits a fragrance like flowers and sweet scented herbs . . . . that is your success.*
> Henry David Thoreau

Without regular shop hours, Jim and Dee are free to tend their plants, host workshops, make presentations and demonstrations, and support area festivals. They are available to the steady stream of visitors who, guided by their newsletter, find Honey Rock (named for a folksong titled *There's Honey in the Rock*).

The Browns' advice to others is "to start slowly and find your niche." With no complaints, they feel it difficult to separate work from play and ponder how they will know when to retire.

Is Bigger Better? The Decision to Expand

Many of the real-life stories sprinkled throughout this book will help answer this awesome question of whether or not bigger is better. There are many who deliberately choose to maintain a one-person small business, garden-based and contained in a garage or porch, on a part-time basis. Even though such individuals may realize full well their enterprise could take off, pulling them along for a wild ride, the decision to have a modest income, a pleasant pursuit, and full control of their personal lives has won out over fame and fortune.

Enlarging a business requires more hours, greater stamina, additional space and help, a mounting overhead with larger payroll and insurance, an inventory that can support all this, and perhaps the assistance of a banker, an accountant, a lawyer, and other professionals.

If such prospects stagger you, think it all over carefully before plunging in. For instance, initiating a tearoom can be appealing. Herb tea parties are such a lovely civilized thing to do. If it's been a part of your overall goal, then go for it.

For many years we served herb tea free and informally. Then our third daughter, Nancy, acquired the property next door and we jumped at the chance to expand. Suddenly we were faced with the additional investment in chairs, tables, china, linen, silverware, and teapots — to say nothing of tea cozies and all the other niceties that make the ladies flock.

Now, because we are into food service, the kitchen must pass inspection (annually), we need auxiliary lighting and ramps for the handicapped, the doors had to be reset to open out, and additional help is necessary for tea party preparation and service. If your facility is large enough, two restrooms may be required. Three years later, we have at last settled into Nancy's addition to our business and are pleased to have it, but for a long while we pondered whether "bigger is better." Since the tearoom requires full-time management, we are fortunate to have Nancy overseeing this entire expansion.

We would love to grow all our own herbs, but I now realize we are lucky — lack of space prohibits taking on this additional workload. Greenhouses require great care, a massive expenditure for heat in our hardiness zone, and, undoubtedly, additional skilled help. It is a demanding business so we have developed good relationships with several local greenhouses. We are happy that our herb plants are just a phone call away, allowing us to concentrate on other projects. The prospect of potting up five thousand seedlings is no longer as much fun as it once seemed.

A herb business can take over a whole house — creativity in the basement, drying in the attic, office space in the den, workshops in the kitchen, sales in the garage. After a number of years conducting a business that has slowly expanded throughout your entire home, bigger would certainly seem better.

You might well consider buying another place with all the space you need. A building with an apartment or office to rent out (income to help pay your mortgage) is a plus. That's what we did. Of course, before approaching your banker and an accountant, go over your figures very carefully to be sure that getting bigger this way is really better. You will need to plot your business' future course on paper, carefully itemize all expenses, and list your goals over a five- and ten-year period.

It's always satisfying to enlarge the scope of your operation. Even if bigger isn't always better, it looks good and the world will nod its approval. To the public, you are proof that the American dream is alive and well. But if you are in debt, can't meet your payroll and rent, or worse, can't pay your taxes, spend sleepless nights trying to keep up, and develop unexplainable health problems, retrench. Relax your grip and go back to what you enjoyed doing to begin with. You may well later ascend the same plateau where you stressed out, but this time the climb will be more gradual and you'll be wiser. You should enjoy your venture into the business of herbs, bigger or smaller.

Bigger is better only if you can cope. Time and time again, as the business stories included attest to, customers have led the way to an enlarged business in a natural progression. Or, the owner deliberately decided to stop at a certain level, perhaps to return to the garden where it all began. It is a wise person who knows his capabilities and can limit his desires. If you plan to enjoy a small one-person business, no one will fault you. Do only what you truly enjoy and no doubt you will be envied for having found your niche in life. You will, as the great Pavarotti says, "sing from the heart."

On the other hand, this is a business with extraordinary potential. If you want it all and are not destroyed by pressure, then bigger will definitely prove better. Be fearless! Pursue greatness! The entire world of herbs, all of us, will benefit from your endeavors.

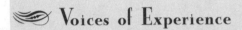 **Voices of Experience**

Countryside Samplings
Alice M. Prall

A gravel pit on their Pennsylvania property inspired the Pralls to try growing herbs; the herbs thrived in the dry stony soil. As the garden grew, Alice Prall looked for outlets to market the produce. First, she sold fresh-cut herbs to restaurants. The demand for plants got the business off and running. Experimenting with drying and crafting with the herbs, Alice expanded the business in this direction. Several years later, Alice realized she was working two full-time jobs. With family encouragement (and with fear and trembling), she left her job as a graphic artist to run the business full-time.

By Countryside Samplings' seventh year, Alice realized the business was as large as she could handle. In the belief that bigger is not always better, Alice decided to keep the business small, independent, and home-based. She feels her business remains unique, offering customers a personal touch and the assurance of quality goods.

Tending the gardens, operating the gift shop, running year-round workshops and classes, and offering lectures and demonstrations keep Alice Prall's schedule as full as she wants it to be. Consignments or outside rentals don't appeal to her. "I am totally happy doing my own thing by myself," says Alice.

BERTOLDI'S CEDAR HILL GARDENS
DAVID AND DEBORAH BERTOLDI

When Deborah Bertoldi got tired of hearing her husband mutter, "This place is starting to look like a business or a real expensive hobby," another home-based garden enterprise was born.

Calling herself a "professional DIRT person," Deborah spent several years talking to others in the business, taking every course she could, and marketing door-to-door while romping in the sunshine with her growing family.

With expanded gardens and product line, Cedar Hill Gardens supplied the public in the Reading, Pennsylvania area with fresh organic produce, fresh-cut herbs, and cut-your-own bouquets, dried flowers and herbs, fresh eggs, and organic meat along with "a gardening experience you'll never forget." Every year their business expanded until it got out of hand. More and more customers, more and more phone calls, more and more demands — what to do about this cute little garden business? They decided to move up with the Big Boys, but they needed help.

> *Those who labour in the earth are the chosen people of God.*
> Thomas Jefferson

Being a big, strong five foot two, Deb drew herself up to full size and over a two-year period organized a co-op of serious organic growers who love the business as much as she does. By directing and drawing on the talents of five other strong gardeners, Deborah's endeavor has helped take pressure off all of them. The co-op also accepts organically grown bounty from others.

In spring, they sell fifty varieties of herbs and one hundred varieties of perennial plants. Everyone pitches in to turn out all their market demands. And demanding it is. They spend long, hard days in the field but find it fulfilling.

Deborah says, "Most of my inspiration is the simple pleasure of watching the miracle of plants grow."

WHAT IS SUCCESS?

Define success! Each of us will have a different view. For some it will be a fat profit, the bottom line. For others it will be a busy lifestyle exuding the satisfaction that comes from introducing others to the wonders of herbs. There are those who will settle for the prestige of being known as the expert. My success is a combination of all of the above wrapped up in happiness in what I am doing. It is its own reward.

Success comes in many forms. If profit is your motive and you are an audacious business person with masterful managerial skills, you will undoubtedly achieve great financial success. This is a relatively young business with great diversity panting to be developed in any number of directions.

In his garden every man may be his own artist without apology or explanation. Each within his green enclosure is a creator, and no two shall reach the same conclusion; nor shall we, any more than other creative workers, be ever wholly satisfied with our accomplishment. Ever a season ahead of us floats the vision of perfection and herein lies its perennial charm.
Louise Beebe Wilder

A number of years ago, a man called one Sunday and pleaded to see The Rosemary House. "We are in the area and my wife wants to start a small herb business," he said. I regretted my kindness when I came in from watering our garden and found him copying down source addresses from files in the back room. As they left, I overheard him say to his wife, "If you are going to do this, you are going to do it right."

In no time, I encountered him at a gift show wholesaleing a vast line of fragrances since found in every drugstore and supermarket across the country. His wife's little herb garden and dreams of a small shop were buried under huge warehouses, herbal factories, and shipping docks. He was buying herbs by the carload and shipping out manufactured products by the truckload. I often wondered how much his wife was enjoying his success.

On the other hand, there is Rosetta Fridley of N-Tangle-Mint herb garden. Her home came already designed for such a business with a street-level basement shop that leads directly out to her lovely herb gardens. By the door there's a pile of charming herb bunches tied with ribbons, hand-sewn fragrant sachet bags, and see-through containers filled with dried flower heads, seed pods, lamb's-ears leaves, and many colorful delights. "Those are free for children to take," she explains in passing. I longed to be a child again.

Her entire backyard is given over to herbs with only grass paths to move from here to there. Out in front, along the curb, is a pile of surplus divided perennials marked "Free." "I took out an old wisteria along the fence," says Rosetta, "and it fell into three pieces. Just then three people came along and each took one. Wasn't I lucky?"

For every purchase I made, she pressed into my hand something else I admired, free. When we walked the garden, she carried her spade. A word from my lips quickly produced a piece for my garden. "Oh, Rosetta," I protested, "you'll never make money this way." "But I'm so happy," was the soft reply. And that is her success. Generously sharing the hobby she obviously adores.

Anyone who has become self-sufficient and can be counted master of their life can measure their success by any standard. Keeping goals in mind and moving toward them in an orderly progression will accomplish your vision, whatever that may be, and with that, success is yours.

Chapter 5

MARKETING AND PUBLIC RELATIONS

MAKE A NAME FOR YOURSELF

YOUR NAME — both your business name and your personal name — is one of your greatest assets. Select a name for your business before you open — a name that is both descriptive of what you do and memorable.

Choosing a name can be tricky, take your time deciding. Avoid names that are easily mispelled or too hard for the average person to pronounce, remember, or understand. There are a great many Herb Barns, Herb Shops, Herb Farms out there. To avoid confusion consider adding your own name: i.e., Smith's Herb Barn, Jane Jones' Herb Shop, Good's Herb Farm. There is nothing wrong with using the magic word HERB in the name — it spells it out, so to speak. Although "The Rosemary House" was perfectly clear to me, we have spent a great deal of time answering a lot of questions about our name. Not everyone ties it to herbs, I have learned to my dismay. Most people just assume my name is Rosemary. Had I realized this problem, I would have legally changed my name twenty-five years ago. Now we try to rectify our problem by adding a tag line — "Your one stop herb shop."

Once you've settled on a name, use it on everything you sell, in every business transaction you conduct, and in every piece of promotional material you send out or give to anyone. Building name recognition is extremely important to business success.

Equally important to your business name is your personal name — particularly in a small business where you want to promote the feeling of personalized service and caring. Your herb business is unique — let people know who is at the heart of the business.

When we first opened The Rosemary House, I was so intimidated by the transformation from mother to shopkeeper that I hid behind the name "Rosemary." Everything but checks was signed or answered as "Rosemary." It wasn't until my first book was published under my given name that I came out of hiding and began to use it again. But, sometimes I still sign "a.k.a. Rosemary" after my signature.

Worse than using only your business name is using no name. Nothing frustrates me more than a communication with no apparent author. Use your given name, make it loud and clear. Be bold! Don't make people guess "who wrote this?" or "who owns this shop?" or "where can I buy this?" or "who is teaching this workshop?" or "who made these wreaths?" Employ your greatest asset, a good name, free yet beyond price.

Be sure your name is part of every flyer, every events schedule, every inquiry that you launch. If there's room for it on your shop sign, well and good.

It is a big mistake not to use your name in every connection to the business you are developing. The association can be to your advantage. This simple fact took me years to learn, which I regret. But you don't need to make the same mistake. Don't be bashful, use your greatest single asset — your given name — every chance you get, from the minute you first open your door for business.

CREATE AN IMAGE

As you harvest your herbs and prepare them for your shop shelves, before you know it you'll be deciding how to package, display, and sell your wares. It's important — even at these early stages when you may be working with just a few products and limited resources — to create an image that's attractive and consistent. This doesn't have to be fancy, but it deserves some thought. If you develop a strong "look" early on, and, even better, a logo or recognizable design element that you can use on your labels, packaging, and letterhead, then you'll be further along in creating a business that people remember and come back to time and time again. Furthermore, distinctive packaging and labeling of your product is essential in guiding the customer as to what she or he is looking at, and what it contains and how it's used.

PACKAGING FOR "OUR LOOK"

"What in the world are you going to do with all those ribbons?" the salesman asked me. "Just you wait and see. Ribbons will be our image," I said. And so they have become.

Back in 1968, when we first started The Rosemary House, we packaged everything in clear baggies tied with perky bows. It was all we could afford.

Everything was color coded: blue for rosemary, yellow for lemon verbena, pink for rosebuds, and so forth. We mounted a little chart in the workroom and added others as needed — rust for cedarwood, brown for cinnamon, apricot for linden tea. Our ribbon assortment expanded with our inventory.

Your packaging can be as simple as a baggie tied with a colored bow.

Baskets, wooden boxes, and other old containers also piled up to hold our color-coded baggies of herbs and spices and teas. It was a downright colorful array, no doubt about it. As I had predicted, it became "our look." A dear friend who frequently helps measure, label, and tie bows announced, "I shall write the story of The Rosemary House and call it Baggies and Bows!" This simple, effective device is still very much in evidence. We have since adopted printed labels but even some of those are attached to the package with bows. Old habits, especially user-friendly ones, are hard to shed.

In the beginning we hand-wrote our labels, but eventually we were able to copy them at our local quick-print shop, which saved a lot of time. As finances allowed, we were able to develop professional-looking typeset labels with appropriate artwork to grace our products.

Our first printed label was a small two- by three-inch generic blank with our "The Rosemary House" logo and "every herb bearing seed" written across the bottom. Still in existence, these are handy for odds and ends that don't have a proper label.

We have also developed pretty folded tag labels that tie onto large items such as wreaths, acting as a handwritten label and price tag, and doubling as a free gift card. A new label is always exciting. Size, shape, color, how to attach it are group decisions made after much staff discussion.

We have about 200 different labels for our various herbs, potpourris, vinegars, crafts, and many other products. Our labels are designed by many artists, sometimes people we haven't even met. When an attractive handwritten order catches our eye, we put out a query and if the writer agrees, we provide them with details of our next label and they design it. We "pay" them with a gift certificate attached to our catalog.

We have also developed a series of Mail-A-Herb cards, our own copyrighted cards that include a package of lavender, patchouli, zebrovka, mint, catnip, lunaria (or money plant), rosemary, bay, or camomile. They are enormously popular because the attractively printed folders contain recipes, history, and other useful

Develop a variety of labels and cards to fit your range of products.

information as well as a generous sample of the herb. It becomes a small mailable gift/card that's fun to send and to receive, read, and use.

Developing new packaging and labeling represents a giant step forward for any herb business. At The Rosemary House, new packaging creates a new product, in our estimation, even if it is something we have marketed since day one. The customer certainly perceives it this way. Besides elevating a simple product to professional status, packaging and labeling create an opportunity to give customers recipes, uses for the herb, as well as the information required by law, such as contents, and amount or weight.

LABELING

Herbs are generally marketed safely as foods without warning labels. As long as the manufacturing areas are sanitary and you comply with regulations regarding the labeling of contents and weight on the package, there should be no problems. Many will be comforted to know that producers with annual food sales under $50,000 need not comply with the latest FDA nutrition labeling act.

Weight can be given in grams (for costly saffron), ounces, or pounds (as in the case of most herbs), contents can also be described by amount (the exact number of nutmegs or cinnamon sticks, or the number of cups, including half-cups for potpourris). We have been told by our government inspector that all of these are acceptable as proper descriptions of weights and measures.

Ingredient lists can contain everything in your product, from a single herb, if that's the case, to simply "herbs and spices" if you are marketing a house blend with secret ingredients. Salt, sugar, MSG, and any nonherbal ingredient should be listed as a courtesy to consumers on special diets.

You may want to look into copyrighting for your labels. Write to the Copyright Office, Library of Congress, Washington, D.C. 20059, for current information. We copyright all our important original labels, both the artwork and the information. It's a valuable safeguard. Occasionally a letter from our lawyer has convinced "copycats" to discontinue the use of a look-alike label. One had even gone so far as to use our little house logo. That was an astonishing infringement.

Although we have come a long way from those first simple baggies and bows, they're still our first love, still in service, still part of our ambience. When excess cash becomes available we *may* — repeat, *may* — call in a packaging expert for an analysis and state-of-the-art design. But it's not a Rosemary House priority.

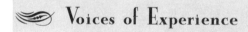 ## Voices of Experience

MARYLAND'S HERB BASKET
MARYLAND MILES MASSEY

In a burst of patriotism, Maryland Miles Massey's parents named her for the state she represents so well. "Made in Maryland" is stamped on her merchandise, and her car license announces MDHERBS.

A registered nurse, Maryland is deputy health officer at the Kent County Health Department in Chestertown. She operates her herb cottage, Maryland's Herb Basket, on Saturdays, her day off.

Maryland and her husband first considered buying the cottage thirty years ago but decided it was too small; instead, they bought the larger twelve-room Victorian next door. But later, they ended up buying the dilapidated little cottage after all! Now Maryland's Herb Basket, the cottage is an ongoing renovation and gardening project.

Maryland bubbles with enthusiasm when she speaks of herbs. Lecturing garden clubs and women's groups, she calls her talk "Herbal Verbals." Maryland has devised her own private-label tea blends: Anniversary Tea (raspberry leaves, blue malva flowers, and rosemary for remembrance); Holiday Tea (apple and cinnamon chips with lavender for pure joy); Sunshine Tea (lemon verbena, lemon balm, and calendula for cheerfulness).

Besides the tea blends, her specialties include a delightful Maryland potpourri that bears a state flag label, t-shirts and aprons with the logo, and customized "Maryland with Pride" gift baskets. All her products are also featured in her mail-order catalog.

LADYBUG PRESS
LANE FURNEAUX

Heavenly Herbs — Enjoy Them! is Lane Furneaux's creation, a colorful cookbook with a frisky ladybug traipsing through the book that has sold thousands of copies.

Lane began growing, studying, and using herbs to improve her cooking skills. In a burst of energy, she decided to initiate a Fresh Herb Celebration Week at an area shopping center. Her challenge was to convince over two hundred merchants to participate by featuring herbs or a herb-related initiative, i.e., getting the hardware store to offer a discount on sage green paint. But there was a snag — one large chain would only promote products carried by *all* their stores.

Agonizing over this dilemma for several sleepless nights produced the *Heavenly Herbs Cookbook*. Lane developed it and printed five hundred copies, which were marketed by the chain and fifty of the merchants. She sold out the first week. Lane's lecturing career as "The First Lady of Herbs" in Texas took off.

Ladybugs, acknowledged by environmentalists as hard workers and considered good luck to boot, now crawl over Lane's business card and stationery. She wholesales and retails her charming cookbook. With but a single booklet to sell, Lane doesn't think others would call her business a booming success, but it makes her lectures more profitable.

Lane has been published by the Royal Horticulture Society in England as well as closer to home. Another of her claims to fame is that she prepared eloquent, nostalgic tussie mussies for the Queen of England and for First Lady Nancy Reagan. "I am never surprised when herbs bring about miracles," says Lane.

DON'T KEEP IT A SECRET

Once you open your doors, scream it from the rooftops — "We are open for business!" Who wants to throw a party and have no one come? Invite the paying public into your new enterprise with every ordinary or unusual way you can employ.

We opened with a bang by advertising in the newspaper, posting flyers in laundromats and supermarkets, and hand writing personal invitations to everyone on our Christmas card lists. I'll never forget opening weekend. We knew the world was ready for this little herb business that we believed in so passionately, and the crowds were our proof. It was exhilarating! But it did not prepare us for the trickle of business that followed. Time and publicity have changed all that.

PAID ADVERTISING

When you think of publicizing your business, advertising probably comes to mind first — and it certainly has an important role in getting the word out. But paid advertising is expensive.

Our one ongoing advertising expense is for a listing under "HERBS" in the Yellow Pages of the telephone book. We know this is a well-used resource — we use it to find herb businesses wherever we travel in the United States. You can purchase an ad through the phone company; billing is usually monthly at a modest rate.

When business is good, it pays to advertise; when business is bad, you've got to advertise.
Anonymous

We have an advertising budget which we spend carefully, trying to adhere closely to its limits. Our purchases are made in all the local newspapers, and in several herb-oriented magazines and newsletters. The greatest proportion of our budget is reserved for ads in the largest city newspaper covering the greatest area adjacent to our business location.

We have learned that, bar none, this assures us the widest audience and best attendance at the events we advertise. Although advertising is the lion's share of our open house budgets, we have learned ways to augment the paid advertising with other less expensive means and free publicity.

If you are in an out-of-the-way location, advertising is key. You will need a rack card for every motel and tourist attraction in the vicinity. Advertise in all the tourist industry promotions, usually a seasonal magazine paid for by the ads and distributed free. Consider this as important as rent and include it in your operating budget. Remember to include the word HERBS, big and bold, in all your ads. The word is a magnet to both aficionados and novices.

FREE AND LOW-COST AVENUES

Sponsoring special events that are free to the public entitles you to a free listing on many public calendars. These require that you mail out press releases by their specified deadline (usually two weeks to three months in advance). A press release must contain all the pertinent information — where, when, who, what, why, and fee or free. It should be short (no more than one page in most cases), typed, doubled-spaced on your letterhead or a plain white sheet of paper. "For Immediate Release" should appear at the top and be sure to include your name and phone number so the editor can check back with you for further information. A word of advice: Always send your press releases separately from any advertising information you may be sending. Otherwise the release may be confused and printed as an ad — and then you have a bill to pay. Be imaginative and persistent in exploring every avenue for free listings, including public service announcements on local TV and radio stations.

Occasionally we get newspaper coverage for one of our important special events. Sometimes an advance mailing of a photograph of our honored guest or some other unusual angle about the program will appeal to an editor. Cultivate connections with your local newspaper editor. We have found it worthwhile to also send short press releases to the editors and writers for the "Business Briefs," food, and gardening sections. Constant vigilance in sending out releases and maintaining contacts earns us extra listings we couldn't afford to buy. One of our most effective forms of free publicity is an "Ask Us" column offered by the newspaper where readers are invited to send in their questions; any about herbs and spices, get our personal attention and response in print.

Don't overlook radio or television opportunities either. Send all your news releases to the news editors and special program hosts of your area stations. The payoff may be a mention — or sometimes you may even be invited to make a personal appearance. Cooking shows, gardening programs, and local news are often open to program suggestions. Don't be shy. If you're invited, go! We have appeared regularly on several local TV and radio shows, and demonstrated the magic of herbs to a wide audience that we couldn't have reached as effectively (or affordably!) on our own.

We willingly lecture at a reduced rate to groups within a fifty-mile radius of our shop because it counts as advertising — these are people we want to attract to the shop. For events sponsored by an outside organization, always request that they publicize the meeting in the local media, and insist that they mention your business name — and spell it right! This type of advertising is much more effective than any you can buy.

For a book signing, a garden party, our "Twice-a-TwelveMonth" open house parties, and the fairy festival, we always print inexpensive flyers. These are hand-distributed — stuffed in customers' bags at our shop, stacked at the local bank and library, posted on supermarket bulletin boards, taken along to every lecture or workshop, mailed to nearby retirement villages, and generally forced on everyone we meet.

Printed brochures, flyers, and cards have many uses. With rising postage rates, mailing can be expensive, though effective, so you need to consider the benefits versus the costs. You can build your own mailing lists. Over the years, we have invited visitors, customers, workshop attendees, my students at Harrisburg Area Community College, and everyone attending our open house parties to sign our list.

As in a letter to a friend, a mailing is a grand person-to-person way to let interested people know what you are doing. The more personal the better. Your customers become an extended family of friends. It's not only a good way to keep them informed about exciting happenings but also to chat about specials in the shop, to offer discounts such as a two-for-one plant sale, or to enclose a gift coupon. "Cut and bring this in by the end of the month" can lure customers for a free sachet, packet of herb seeds, or a surplus plant.

A business card is essential. Include as much information as possible: the name of your business, of course; your name too as you want it to be known; hours of operation; the address; directions (perhaps a little map);

HERBS loud and clear; a list of what you plan to sell (wreaths, plants, books, antiques, herbal crafts, vinegars); and your logo. Use both sides, double-folded, if need be. An attractive informative standard-size two- by three-and-a-half-inch business card is a goal and an asset. I would even advise investing in the services of a professional card designer; it could be your best spent dollars.

Don't go anywhere, ever, even to church, without your events schedule or business brochures or, at the minimum, your business card. Take them along to club meetings, organizations, summer camp, daycare or senior centers, shopping, wherever you go, day or night, even to parties. It can be a handy icebreaker.

Make your business card an effective marketing tool by packing it with information on both sides.

If someone asks you what you do, be prepared to whip out your business card in a twinkling. If they don't ask, bring it up anyway. People respond when you share and it's good for business too. You are your own best advertising, so don't be modest. Crow about your unique enterprise and make everyone want to come see it.

DON'T BE SHY — SPEAK UP!

For most people, facing an audience falls somewhere in the realm with hanging. Polls show public speaking is the number-one fear among Americans. If this is true for you, it's time to put all that behind you. Realize you are your business's best advertisement: telling people about your business face to face is the surest way to draw them into your tent (or shop).

When invitations to speak on the subject of herbs appear on your doorstep (and they will), be determined to conquer your fear and win over your audience. Trust me, it can be done.

First of all, speak only about herbal things you have mastered — whether it be gardening, cooking with herbs, home remedies, or crafts you have learned to make from your garden. You will be most comfortable talking about topics you actually enjoy.

To be an effective speaker, organize your presentation to include an introduction, your main points, and a brisk ending within the time allotted. Be sure to use a light touch, a bit of humor to keep them interested, and be sure to nod your head occasionally. When you see your audience nodding back, you know they are with you.

I always pack a few baskets of herbal items to show and tell, and perhaps to sell. These props become my notes, and add a visual element to my presentation. They provide something the audience can relate to and understand, and make it easy for me to explain what it is, how to grow it, how to make it, or how to use it. Afterward, people love to come up to see, touch, and smell the display.

Every time you experiment with a new recipe or devise another way to package an old one, tuck it into your traveling basket of goodies for the next lecture. Before you know it, you will find yourself developing the next presentation. This helps keep your enthusiasm level high, with new angles to talk about as the year progresses.

When you have a shop, it's easy to take along display items that will sell as well, a real bonus for the time and work you put into the presentation. With such a captive audience, I either offer a small discount or contribute a percentage of my sales to the organization's pet project. People who come to The Rosemary House after a presentation look at our things with new respect and better understanding.

I always like to offer my audience something free. This can be last year's seeds, a photocopied herb chart, popular salt-free recipes, or a tablespoon of the fragrant potpourri I whipped up before their very eyes. Make certain your shop's name, address, and hours are on your free gift for therein lies the best advertising of all. People will keep your little freebie, remember your fascinating talk, and decide to pay you a visit to satisfy lingering curiosity.

For conventions and other large groups, suggest to the sponsor that they offer door prizes and herbal favors purchased from your shop. This agreement will keep your staff busy, enhance your presentation, and increase your income for the day's work.

Dressing for the occasion can be part of the fun, and a way to elevate your psyche to the task. Long skirts, homespun shawls, spice jewelry, or a chaplet of herbs provide good photo opportunities. Gentlemen can wear a top hat, flowing bowtie, craftsman shirt, or even a flamboyant flowing cape to set the mood. We attended one wonderful presentation on old-time medicines where the herbalist dressed the part in a tall hat, frock coat, huge tie, and carried a black bag filled with his tricks. To say his appearance enhanced his presentation is an understatement.

By all means set a fee for your presentation. We shy people hesitate to do this, but if you make the mistake of speaking without compensation, you will find yourself very busy doing more lectures than you will enjoy. My stern advice is: don't hesitate to say, "I have a fee." Establish what it is before you ink the date on your calendar. Increase your fee as your experience and reputation as a speaker grows.

When you feel comfortable on a platform, spread the word of your availability. Contact the program chairpeople of all your local organizations and send your program press release to every convention center within a two- to three-hour radius of your shop. These people are constantly searching for entertainment for their members and guests. Your specialty message is appealing because it will give the audience something to enjoy as well as to think about.

One final tip: Believe wholeheartedly in yourself and your topic. As a spokesperson for herbs, you know that what you have to say is enormously interesting and worthwhile. Remember your initial enthusiasm for herbs? Keep in touch with this as you present, and your audience will respond by listening attentively.

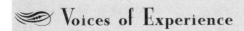 ## Voices of Experience

HERBAL HARVEST FLORAL AND GIFT SHOPPE
JAN BUTLER

Jan Butler's herbal odyssey began when she volunteered to work on an herb farm: she knew immediately that she wanted to do this for the rest of her life.

By the time she settled in Illinois, Jan had her gardens, Herbal Harvests, going strong and was ready to open a shop. She was also teaching herb courses at the local community college. Between her classes and a series of open house parties, plant sales, an annual garden walk, and Christmas events at her shop, Jan developed an extensive mailing list. Soon she developed a newsletter to share herb information with her network.

Jan's gardens continued to grow as she found additional leased land. Upon enrolling in a master's program in horticulture at the University of Illinois, Jan began expanding the gardens two acres a year. She now organizes the Wild Thyme Herbalists program and a herb study group. She also employs three staff members and twenty-five consignment craftspeople in her shop.

Jan has also added a full kitchen so she can offer cooking classes and a daily herbal luncheon program. With a missionary's zeal, she also does TV, radio, and newspaper stories and puts on a herb fair every August. Jan's business has expanded and moved into a 2000-square-foot shop in historic Geneva, Illinois, freeing up her home for living quarters, while she continues to harvest several of the surrounding acres.

ARIE'S HERB GARDENS
PENNY MOORE AND WANDA RAYFIELD

Wanda Rayfield, an eighth-grade English teacher, inspires her students to explore life and literature with indoor lights for plants, a fish aquarium, and even a comfortable rocking chair to sit and read aloud their favorite stories.

A class project on *Foxfire* and an ensuing affection for the strongly independent wise woman, Aunt Arie, inspired Wanda to team up with her colleague Penny Moore to grow herbs in milk carton containers under the lights. Total ignorance did not generate resounding success, but on the other hand they took home six runty basils which flourished in the intense humidity and hundred degree temperatures of an Alabama summer. Having enough basil to make pesto for the entire county triggered Wanda and Penny's abiding interest in herbs.

Undaunted by additional failures, the teachers read everything they could find, planted seeds by every suggested scientific method with more disappointing results, and finally built raised beds filled with well-drained soil which they stocked with plants purchased from nurseries.

Such diligence was rewarded. The partners began marketing fresh-cut herbs to upscale restaurants in Birmingham. Aha!
Success at last. But they realized it was not yet time to send
their letters of resignation to the board of education.

Fascinated by the revelation that herbs can indeed be a
source of income as well as pleasure, our entrepreneurs continued to read and learn with renewed zest. Now making herbal
products, they have developed a line of bath and culinary herb
items that they purvey at craft shows in their free time.

Arie's is stationed in a small shop in front of Penny's home.
They are selling both wholesale and retail, and developing
consumer interest in herbs through programs to organizations.
Educating the public comes easily to these two teachers.

Penny says they have learned a lot. She writes: "No part
of the herb business is quick or easy, but the successes at-
tained satisfy the very soul. We will never be millionaires, but
the profits we make are sweetened by the knowledge that we
earned them by our own toil and determination. Encouraged
by customer interest, we work toward fulfilling a niche
worthy of the accolades of such an imposing figure as Aunt
Arie herself."

NEWSLETTERS

Regular communication between your business and your customers is
essential to boost business. Whether you produce a monthly reminder
on a one-page typed sheet or a quarterly with a fancy multicolored,
computer-designed layout, you can make your name a household word.
Either will boost sales, fill classes, convey your message, and keep your
name before the public — or at least that sector interested in your
specialty.

An active mailing list that includes the names of regular workshop
attendees, customers, and prospects met at lectures or craft fairs is essential
and should be guarded. With this, you are ready for direct marketing. Mail
notices of your upcoming classes and watch them fill up like magic.

The newsletter is also the place to advertise shop or garden specials,
print a money-saving coupon, and publish hints, tips, and recipes for
using your products. Offer invitations to special events that are fun and

fascinating — a great chance for you to rub elbows with all kindred spirits, your customers. Invite them and they will join you for enlightening events year-round — from May Day to summer solstice and on to winter holiday parties.

You can personalize your newsletter heavily with family and customer anecdotes, or pictures of your cat in the catnip. Give it a cheery name — for a brief period ours was *Ms. Rosemary's Sampler* — and maintain a handy file where you collect bits and pieces to put in it.

Your newsletter might take the form of a herb letter, a teaching tool that also sells anything you want to push. This can be as simple as a recipe for herb butter using dill, or for something more exotic such as homemade curry powder containing twenty different spices. There's a salesman's old maxim: Selling is teaching and teaching is selling. Remember that as you put your newsletter together.

Newsletters are primarily a form of advertising and are deductible as such. Some newsletters — even though they are blatant advertising — charge a subscription fee, usually a modest amount to underwrite postage and printing costs. My only problem with this is that when I forget to renew, I'm dropped off the list. I'm sure a great many people have this same problem with annual renewal, and the publisher inadvertently loses readers.

Your skills and budget will determine the answers to a lot of questions you may have about developing a company newsletter. If your fingers itch at the sight of a blank sheet of paper and a pen, then writing a newsletter may well be your calling. Consider it. Remember that you will face deadlines, especially when you charge a subscription fee and promise a certain number of issues per year. Deadlines always seem to coincide with personal crises, illness in the family, or hectic schedules. Whatever the reason, the heavy pressure that results can be unpleasant.

On the other hand, nothing else builds public relations, spreads goodwill, and mounts profits like a newsletter. With proper planning and organization, it is an effective way to use your knowledge and share herbal experiences.

If you cannot open a retail sales shop for whatever reason, newsletters are an excellent way to go. You can conduct your entire business through the mail; as your mailing list grows, so will sales. A chatty newsletter filled with ways to use your garden herbs can generate a fair amount of sales, and grow into a substantial business over time.

Learn to Make Bows

You may not believe this, but the world will beat a path to the door of a bow maker, even more so than to one who has a better mousetrap. It amazes me that bows have such appeal and that the bow maker is regarded with awe. Develop this simple skill and your herbal enterprise will fly to new heights of success.

We use bows to tie merchandize together into a higher priced package, to transform "losers" into "winners," or to dress up the distressed merchandize that we contribute as prizes for local causes. We also sell bows ready-made.

Sometimes a simple shoelace bow, tied like your sneakers, is the most sophisticated. We do all our baggies this way. It's certainly the easiest and quickest bow. By using several strands of raffia in a shoelace tie, you automatically have loops.

For a fancier multi-looped look, I offer the following illustrated instructions. It is important that the bow always be in scale with the project — narrow ribbon for small items, super-wide ribbon for large baskets. In addition, you should always keep some narrow ribbon on hand for tying the bow loops together (as illustrated), creating a uniform and perky look.

"Practice makes perfect" is the slogan to adopt about bow making. Reuse old ribbons until you've gotten the hang of it, but don't allow yourself to be defeated by bows. Keep saying, "I am the master," and success is yours. It is well worth learning.

1. Tie and knot a 10" piece of narrow ribbon around the item or baggie of herbs you are putting the bow on. (Fig. 1-A) In the case of a gift box or basket, tie the piece wherever the wide ribbons on the box cross. (Fig. 1-B)

This tie will be ready to receive your finished bow (step 3), acting like a second pair of hands when you get there.

For wreaths, bouquets, and other crafts: You may want to substitute a piece of thin wire or pipe cleaner for the narrow ribbon to catch the loops. This gives you a stem that can be easily secured in the finished piece.

Wire or pipe cleaner works particularly well with bulky ribbons such as wide velvet or flocked ribbon, and for nosegays where it can be easily wrapped around the flower stems.

2. Cut a 1- to 3-yard piece of your selected bow ribbon (at least as wide as the narrow piece used in step 1). Hold the tail of the ribbon between your forefinger and thumb, and loop the ribbon up and down in a figure-eight pattern as many times as you like (for the desired number of loops),

catching each loop tightly between your forefinger and thumb. (Fig. 2) Make sure that the right side of the ribbon faces out on all your loops (especially for satin, calico, moire, or velvet).

The secret to success at this stage is to pinch or crease the loops as you go, reducing the width of the "knot spot" to its smallest dimension and, in effect, pre-tying the bow in your hand.

A note on loops: Loops can be uniform in size, creating a pompon effect, or graduated for a more tailored look. Sometimes loops seem to have a will of their own and go in all directions, adding a casual look that still seems to be appreciated by non-bow makers.

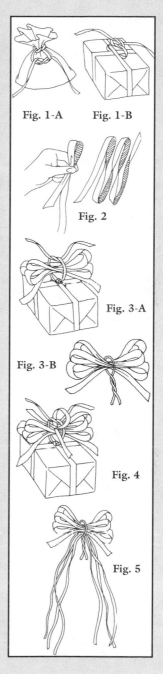

Fig. 1-A   Fig. 1-B

Fig. 2

Fig. 3-A

Fig. 3-B

Fig. 4

Fig. 5

3. Place the loops between the ends of the waiting narrow ribbon on your package and tie tightly. (Fig. 3-A) Or, if you're using wire or pipe cleaner, wrap the piece tightly around the central "knot spot." (Fig. 3-B) The loops will pop up to make a full and perky bow.

4. If you want to cover the knot, cut another 10" piece of your bow ribbon and form it into a small loop. Use the ends of the narrow piece of ribbon to tie this additional loop into place over the knot. (Fig. 4)

5. To add streamers, cut several additional lengths of bow ribbon, of the length and amount you consider graceful. Place them behind your loops before securing the bow in the narrow tie-on piece or wire. (Fig. 5) Once tied, adjust the bow, pull the loops apart, arrange the streamers, and cut the tails into attractive lengths.

Streamers are particularly attractive on bows for nosegays, which I often make with many loops and streamers of narrow ribbon held together with wire.

I think of a herbal newsletter floating through my mailslot as a letter from a friend. I always set it aside to enjoy at leisure — like dessert. Reading one is a sure cure for rainy day doldrums.

BERRY HILL PRESS
DODY LYNESS

Never intending to turn her talent for floral design into a business, Dody Lyness zig-zagged her way into a thriving publishing enterprise. Piqued by the aromatic plants in her garden in Palos Verdes, California, Dody developed an expertise in potpourri making, leading her to teach courses on the subject at a community college, and to write a book, *Potpourri — Easy as One, Two, Three!* This lively paperback, revised four times, is sold in herb shops nationwide.

Dody also launched a quarterly, free, one-page newsletter entitled *Potpourri Party-Line*, giving recipes and announcing sales in each issue. This newsletter, now called *The Flora-Line*, is sold by subscription to dried floral and fragrance designers and numbers twenty pages. Dody is kept busy selling subscriptions, writing and soliciting articles, securing advertising, and meeting deadlines for this major enterprise.

TAILOR YOUR MARKETING
ACTIVITIES TO THE SEASON

As you have probably figured out by now, marketing never stops. Sales fluctuate according to the seasons, and so must our product, special events, and in-house operations. The herb business is especially season-specific: what we have on our shelves varies with the growing season, the holidays, and what's going on in our customers' lives. Tailoring your product to the seasons can really boost your business — and keep you and your staff busy and having fun. The following outline suggests activities for each of the twelve months. It should help you and your staff plan ahead — and, hopefully, generate many more ideas for making the most of seasonal pro-motions and special events. Keep a file of your ideas. As the years progress, watch your files grow along with your products, events — and sales.

A YEAR IN THE HERB BUSINESS

JANUARY

New Year! — A good time to close for vacation. If you don't need a rest from the holidays and the year's labors, then it's time to take inventory, hold sales, restock, reorganize, and sweep.

- I traditionally order seeds on January 1 during the endless football games.
- After Twelfth Night remove all traces of Christmas and get out the Valentines. Red and green bows become red and white or red and pink bows with hearts on wires in the centers. Feature LOVE — Love Tea, Love Bath Balls, Love-in-the-Mist Seeds, heart cookie cutters, and gift baskets of "love."
- This is a good time to offer sales of up to 50 percent off everything in the store, or to lower prices on individual items.
- Time to set up the indoor grow lights and brighten a corner with fresh herb plants.
- Read up on your herbs, then read some more. This is the key to your success and fun to do on a cold, quiet winter's day.

FEBRUARY

Groundhog Day Celebration! — Hold a great winter clearance sale.

Valentine's Day! — Have a celebration, a free party. Serve tea and heart-shaped cookies. Put hearts and red bows on everything. It's a big day for small gift giving.

- The Language of Flowers comes into full play on this romantic day. Dripping with sentiment, the herbs speak eloquently. Make a lacy, sentimental table display with Valentines, sachets, and books on the language of flowers.

Lavender Hearts

- On February 15, think spring and Easter, no matter what the weather. Pack away hearts and red ribbons for another year, spring pastels are in.
- Time to send out your new Events Calendar for the year.

March

The Rites of Spring! — Celebrate by starting seeds. Why not set aside space to sell pots, vermiculite, and seed packets? Celebrate the vernal equinox. Spring will have every gardener's juices flowing. Be ready! For a nominal fee, offer indoor seed-starting classes. Let everyone leave with a recycled pot in a plastic bag, ready to sprout and grow.

- St. Patrick's Day is a relatively minor holiday but pots of shamrocks sell. Offer shoppers free green bows on anything.
- Order plants for resale.
- End of first quarter — already! Pay your quarterly taxes. Do a first-quarter sales analysis.

April

Easter, Passover — Two of the world's great religions are celebrating holidays and herbs are a part of their history. Nesting for Easter baskets, bows, and recipes are free special offerings this month.

- Seeds and herb plants are number-one priority.
- Workshops on how to plant a new herb garden are a timely feature, free with a purchase of $50 worth of plants — or set a fee. Provide a table with graph paper and garden design books, plant lists for theme gardens, pencils, colored pens, rulers, and your advice. Advertise this special spring service.
- The day after Easter begin plans for Mother's Day.
- Secretary's Day, a recent calendar addition, has gained great popularity. Have a supply of small baskets on hand.
- We also push Earth Day, encouraging people to plant nature's air refreshers and natural pesticides.
- Arbor Day is important. Encourage planting herbal trees by giving out free lists. Underwrite a Scout Troop tree planting at a nearby school. (Send the story to the newspaper.)

MAY

A May Pole in the garden will lure visitors. A mossy May basket on the door and Mai-bowle help celebrate May Day.

- ❀ Recognize the fact that Mother's Day is second only to Christmas. Give your best to dear old Mom. She's Queen for the Day and deserves a lovely gift basket of herbs or a fresh tussie mussie from your garden. Advertise and take orders. Serve a festive Mother's Day tea.
- ❀ First harvests: comfrey, lovage, lemon balm, sweet woodruff.

JUNE

We offer our *Twice-A-TwelveMonth Open House* with a featured guest — guaranteed to get us lots of free publicity and draw hundreds of people with delicious herbal food, free recipes, specials, prizes, garden tours, special exhibits, resource table, and herbal videos running continuously in the workshop. Always held the second Saturday in June.

- ❀ Plan a Faerie Festival to celebrate summer solstice.
- ❀ "Gather ye rosebuds" and hold potpourri workshops.
- ❀ Bless the bride — feature weddings in your window. Advertise a coupon special for all brides and those celebrating June anniversaries.

JULY

Get Out the Flag! Dress the window in red, white, and blue. Flags in the garden are lovely.

It's not too soon to think Christmas:

- ❀ Create new merchandise from the burgeoning garden.
- ❀ Design Christmas decorations from lace and bows or twigs and moss.
- ❀ Plan special holiday events.
- ❀ Review your list of ideas, suggestions, reminders from last Christmas.
- ❀ Thinking of Christmas will keep you cool!

August

Summer Doldrums — Unless you are in a tourist area, reduce and clear out all plants, close for vacation to visit other herb shops and gardens. Or . . .

❋ Organize a summer herbal fair. In one small town in Oklahoma where a herb shop did this, the town has now taken over and underwritten this successful Main Street event as their major summer tourist promotion. (*See* Chapter 7, pages 147–149)

Hint: Give your fair a number starting with ONE (i.e., First Annual...). By the time you reach Herb Fair Ten you will hardly be able to contain the crowds, and your business will be a household word.

❋ Do herb gathering in earnest — make vinegars, potpourris, jellies, and teas. Hang the rest.

September

September Days! Salute Senior Citizens — special deals, special events, "Tea and Tussie Mussies" workshops. Collect old-time herbal stories or recipes from their memories or families. Give them free scented geraniums for their winter windowsill in exchange and then print the stories and recipes.

❋ Salute "back-to-schoolers," invite their mommies to tea in the garden. Offer free lunch box recipes for all.
❋ There's a hint of autumn in the air. Celebrate fall equinox with cornshucks and pumpkins, change the window.
❋ Begin to look ahead to the holidays. Stock now! or it will be too late.

October

Harvest! Create herbal wreaths and harvest profits. Teach wreath classes, fresh or dried. Our most popular workshops are dried wreaths — also our most lucrative. People are willing to pay as much to learn how to make a wreath as they will pay for a completed wreath. Clear out a corner for a table and supplies then set workshop dates all through the harvest season. Sell the supplies too.

- Add swags, garlands, and centerpieces to match. Your calendar will be filled.
- Decorate with bales of straw (to be used as mulch when you bed down your garden later) for Halloween. Serve hot mulled cider in an electric cooking pot to celebrate. Be prepared to sell mulling spices.
- Review your Christmas plans and inventory. Slide into gear. It's coming fast. If you haven't already done so, print your holiday flyers with specials, important dates, and a few herbal hints.

Miniature Lace Wreath

NOVEMBER

Give Thanks! Feature pots of herbs for winter windowsill pleasure.

- We hold our second "Twice-a-TwelveMonth" open house with Christmas decorations, scrumptious foods, free recipes using our own herbal seasonings, and a large display of gift baskets to sell or take orders, always the Sunday after Thanksgiving.
- Advent begins. Fresh herbal advent wreaths are a specialty. Take orders or teach classes.
- Christmas now spills out of the back room to erupt, full-blown, in every nook and corner. On the day after Thanksgiving, one of our busiest days, "the fifth season" takes over in earnest. Clear the decks! Deck the decks!

Pressed Herb Ornament

DECEMBER

Holiday Busy-ness. All hands on deck. No time now for special events. Full-time work on packaging products, gift baskets, special orders. This is when it all happens. This one month can equal the other eleven months moneywise. You work toward this all year.

- On December 26 the elves rest . . .
- Until the New Year, order herb seeds and begin the annual cycle all over again, picking up steam and new ideas as you go along. The years mount quickly.

❦ Keep a diary or file with lists and suggestions to guide you through the year. If you have a good idea, jot it down. This is especially helpful for holiday planning.

Voices of Experience

BETSY WILLIAMS / THE PROPER SEASON
BETSY WILLIAMS

As the daughter of authors, Betsy Williams has spent a lot of time reading her favorite myths and fairytales, as a child and to her own children. One year she decided to try growing all the plants she read about in these stories — Peter Rabbit's camomile, Titania's cupid's flower, Mrs. Rabbit's tobacco — and she fell head over heels in love with herb and flower gardening and crafting. In 1969 Betsy began marketing some of her surplus produce.

Guided by the seasons, Betsy spent the winters in horticultural libraries reading and taking notes; the springs planting her seeds; the summers harvesting her crop; and autumns selling her produce. Her sensitivity to the cycle of seasons became the theme for Betsy's new shop, which she acquired upon outgrowing her farmhouse quarters. The Proper Season varies its products and events as the year progresses — each season growing out of the preceding one and contributing to the richness and enjoyment of the next.

Betsy's year climaxes with Christmas, celebrated as a season all unto itself. As Betsy claims, "A month of Christmas is much more fun and satisfying than a day of Christmas!" So from St. Nicholas Day on December 6 to Twelfth Night on January 6th, the shop overflows with handmade ornaments from around the world, boxwood and berry baskets, and a special Wreath of Christmas Legends.

Classes, herbal weddings, a faerie festival in spring, wreaths and arrangements from the garden (fresh or dried), and a mail-order catalog have helped this enterprise prosper and grow.

Chapter 6

The Heart of the Business: Developing Your Product

As you open your market for herbs, it will occur to you that certain items sell better than others. These are the products you will prefer to stock, simply because they sell. However, along the way, as your expertise and your herb garden grow, experiment with other herbal ideas to vary your inventory and entice new customers. Developing appropriate packaging and labeling (*see* page 89) will be your challenge; change it until you hit upon the best way to market a particular product. Here is a whole garden full of potentially profitable ideas — fifty of them — for you to harvest and experiment with. May they keep you busy and prosperous.

50 Profitable Product Ideas

1 **Potpourri** may be overdone, but it is still one of our best sellers. A fragrant, colorful, modestly priced potpourri will enrich your sales. Make huge batches: big bags, little bags, sachets, or enormous bowls full with a handy help-yourself scoop. Give each mixture a romantic name, and keep your inventory level high. Record the recipe as you create a new mixture, so you can duplicate the winners.

2 **Colorful Bags of Ingredients** for do-it-yourselfers are a profitable by-product of the potpourri business. Your surplus harvest will be welcomed by crafters without gardens. One of our best sellers is discarded herb leaves, marketed in plump bags labeled "Potpourri Herbs from the

Garden." As I package this mixture, my husband says in disbelief, "You don't *sell* that stuff?" "Every bit of it," is my reply. In fact, we sell out. To complete your line of bulk spices and potpourri supplies for do-it-yourselfers, you will probably need to carry essential oils, fixatives, and bright blue bachelor's-buttons, dark red peony and poppy petals, golden marigolds, and pretty pink rose petals.

3 **A Potpourri Pet** wearing colorful petals as "fur" makes a most engaging presentation. Made from a topiary form stuffed with sphagnum moss, fragrant potpourri glued on the exterior and suitably bowed, this wide-eyed house pet quietly exudes scent and charm. Occasionally I add a few drops of a favorite oil, which the moss absorbs and holds readily. This pet looks inviting in any shop and is easily replaced when sold. The topiary forms come in many sizes and shapes.

4 **Packaging and Marketing Potpourri** is limited only by your imagination. We devise new packaging daily: jars with lace toppers, baskets, odd cups swathed in a pouff of cellophane, antiques of all sorts, old handkerchiefs, pretty bowls, pottery containers, and boxes galore — clear, heart-shaped, Shaker, homemade. Sachets are probably the most common. Small six-by-six-inch squares of fabric work well for made-to-order favors for conventions or family reunions. We have several women who select fabrics and stitch up potpourri bags in various sizes for the shop. One of our favorites is a snowy white cotton guest towel that holds a quart of the aromatic mixture. Sometimes we use Battenburg lace doilies or scarf squares to make large, puffy sachets. Beribboned, with lots of lace, and decorated with dried or silk flowers, these impressive presentations are extremely profitable.

Sachets made from a variety of laces and fabrics are popular as favors for special occasions or conventions.

5 **Essential Oils** are irresistible. We keep them conveniently stocked at the front desk where we can make suggestions and answer questions. Except for a very few adventurous souls, distilling your own oils is out of the question. In earlier times, distilling oils was a major in-house operation. Experiment if you wish, but I recommend leaving this process to the

professionals. They will provide you with a wide variety of fragrant oils by the pound or in tiny bottles ready for resale. We have been buying and repackaging oils since the day we opened, thanks to a pharmacist friend who obtains them in bulk for us. In fact, he was so relieved that we were doing the packaging, he started referring customers to us who were seeking small amounts of peppermint oil for candy, clove oil for toothache, wintergreen for alcohol rubs, and rose oil for potpourri. We repackage many of our oils, but also sell fragrances that are only available prepackaged. A line of oils for perfume, aromatherapy, or cooking is well worth developing.

6 **Fragrances** of all sorts sell very well. Customers step into The Rosemary House and demand, "How can I make my house smell like this?" Of course, they can't — but they can try! The appealing aura of fragrance is undeniable. My home doesn't smell as wonderful as the shop, despite my best efforts. The shop is like a gigantic potpourri — the smells of hundreds of fragrant herbs and spices, and thousands of products and by-products mingling in an enclosed space, constantly replenished and refreshed with every harvest and incoming shipment. All of this should be your stock in trade — soaps, oils, perfumes, sachets, potpourris, bunches of fresh herbs, pounds of exotic spices, teas, incense, aromatic mixtures — combined, melded, aged together into a medley of scents. It sways the sensibilities. We have been accused of opening our doors and wafting the sweet fragrance across the street to lure customers. But that's mere rumor!

7 **Tea** is nearly synonymous with herbs to many people. Even those who don't enjoy any other use of herbs find many flavors of herbal tea pleasurable. Your garden is a gold mine of golden fragrant brews. Mint tea is the all-time favorite, but there are countless other popular herbal teas. Try them all, and experiment with blends. Devise your own shop specialty. We have a Love Tea especially suitable for shower favors and wedding gift baskets. We also have a popular Shakespearean Tea with "hot lavenders, mints, savory, marjoram" from *The Winter's Tale*. HospitaliTea was blended for a special occasion at a local hospital, and Leo Tea from "The Herb of the Zodiac" was inspired by the birthday of a dear Leo friend. TranquilliTea is a soothing relaxant made from a formula I found in an old book. In honor of the refurbishing of the Statue of Liberty, we composed delicious Ms. LiberTea, containing American native herbs mixed with a few immigrants. We sent some to the celebration's chairman,

Mr. Lee Iaccoca, who wrote us a nice letter of thanks. The tea also garnered us a special celebratory article in the local newspaper.

Don't overlook the value of versatile herb teas. Our garden can produce only so much, so we carry teas from several other reliable sources. In January and February, they outsell everything else we have and are hard to keep in stock. We also encourage sales by serving herbal teas, hot or iced, at all our public events.

8 **Selling Fresh Herbs** to cooks and restaurants offers staggering business potential. In summer, we put out galvanized buckets filled with fat bunches of dill for pickles, or basil for pesto. The crop must be harvested when it comes in, so either sell it fresh to stores or dry what doesn't sell for later use. We can't harvest enough mint for all the Kentucky Derby parties in our area, so we gather it from our friends' gardens as well.

Phone calls, personal visits, or letters to local chefs will open this market up to you if you have a productive garden. We have one restaurant that depends upon our fresh tarragon and French sorrel for their special salmon sauce. A chef at the famous Greenbriar Hotel in West Virginia told me they use $20,000 worth of fresh herbs a year. In our area, come winter, one would need a large greenhouse to fulfill such a contract.

9 **Spices.** Three thousand years later, the world still buzzes over Sheba's delivery of spices to King Solomon. She mounted a fabulous caravan the likes of which the world had never seen, with camels lumbering along at twenty miles a day, each bearing two tons of precious cargo. The spice delivery, along with her feminine wiles, surely got Sheba all she wanted. Spices are no less valuable or useful today than they were in Sheba's day. You should have some in stock.

Some people refer to a herb garden harvest as "spices," and I won't argue with them. However, to complement your herbal harvests you may purchase a line of culinary spices for resale (*see* Sources, page 172). We sell whole cinnamon sticks in every available length, frankincense and myrrh at Christmastime, whole cloves by the pound for pomander makers, vanilla beans, star anise, cardamon pods, whole or ground ginger, peppercorns in five colors, tonka beans for exotic potpourris, and vetiver roots. All of these come from Asia, Africa, and other areas of the tropics, bought in bulk from importers.

10 **Mustards.** In Mt. Horeb, Wisconsin, there is a Mustard Museum and gift shop specializing in — you guessed it — mustard. With 1,397 different varieties to date, the museum lures mustard aficionados and the curious from far and near. Since I never get to that part of our vast country — although thousands have visited the museum — I know about this unique enterprise through its mail-order catalog. The variety is staggering. They sell mustard with dill, caraway, tarragon, horseradish, ginger, Vidalia onion, whisky, beer, champagne, honey, cranberry, spices, papaya, lemon lime, and hot chilis to name a few. Although that's not the whole list, you get the idea of the kinds of gourmet mustard that can be made with minced herbs fresh from the garden or dried if need be. You can make the popular condiment from scratch by mixing mustard powder and vinegar. Because of my demanding schedule, I usually buy a gallon of salad mustard — the kind used freely on hot dogs at ball games — which definitely needs some help. Add your choice of herbs to create a shop specialty.

11 **Make a Mint with Mint!** The mainstay of any herb garden or business, mint is the one herb everyone relates to. Who doesn't know mint-flavored toothpaste or after-dinner mints? (See more on mint in Chapter 1, page 11, and under Lavender on page 9, for almost everything that can be done with lavender can also be done with mint.) Used as an ancient biblical tithe, mint comes in at least twenty-five, well-defined species, and there are over six hundred varieties to sell your customers: spearmint, peppermint, curly mint, apple, pineapple, ginger, variegated, water, orange, Japanese, black-stemmed, Scotch, horsemint, bergamot, lemon, pennyroyal, Corsican, and many more. It's fun to search them out and collect them. Many are crossbred hybrids given common names for convenience. Study mints and you'll discover an entanglemint!

12 **Herbal Jellies** — Don't overlook these jewel-like beauties that grace your shelves. Thanks to commercial pectins, making herbal jelly is easy. Mint with grapefruit juice, sage with grape juice, tarragon and cranberry juice, rosemary in tomato juice, thyme made with orange juice are only some of the flavorful possibilities. My personal favorite is lemon balm jelly with a squeeze of lemon juice to enhance its flavor. It tastes exactly like lemon meringue pie!

These delicious jellies are in great demand. Use the recipe for mint jelly that is always included with pectins as a base, substituting your choice of herbal infusion for the mint. Use any fruit juice as the liquid and follow instructions carefully. We find herb jellies sell quickly in assorted recycled glass containers — brandy snifters, baby food jars, sundae glass dishes, wine goblets, and juice glasses — labeled, of course, and topped with bits of fabric, yarn bows, old lace doilies, and decorative papers. The packaging looks great even though most of it is recycled. In fact, we have a sign offering five cents each for clean baby food jars.

13 **Honey** and all its by-products make a superb product if your herb garden harbors bees and hives. Herbal honey is superior to any other. Along with the honey, you can market candles, ornaments, and pure beeswax. Collect information on the many uses of beeswax to share with your customers. We were fortunate to know a couple with a large herb garden and apiaries. We gladly sold their delectable herbal honey by the pint, quart, and gallon.

14 **Flavored Vinegars** are easy to make, in demand, and always profitable. In Pennsylvania, the state insists upon inspecting kitchens where herbal vinegars are produced and bottled — check out your state's regulations before starting. We find the law unnecessary, since we don't use our kitchen. But all our vinegars for sale are made by a gentleman with an approved kitchen and a very large herb garden. They are brewed in gallon glass jars right out in the sunny garden. The sun beats down on them unmercifully, gently warming the vinegars and extracting herbal oils and flavors. Bottled and labeled appropriately, these vinegars sell quickly. Lavender chive-blossom vinegar, rich

Make your own flavored vinegars in gallon jars, then strain them into smaller decorative bottles for sale.

"dark opal" basil, tarragon, and red raspberry vinegars are our best sellers. We've devised other specialty combinations such as zesty chili pepper and garlic and, our favorite, a colorful rosehip, rose geranium, and rosemary vinegar that we call The Rosemerriest.

15 **Dips** delight today's carefree hostess. Purchase them for resale or devise your own. But be sure to stock dips. Any tasty instant dip is a best seller. "Mix and serve" has become standard fare with today's fast-moving lifestyle. It takes us the better part of a year to devise a new dip, but it is a fun project. We test and revise each recipe many times; customers love doing taste tests and giving us input. Packaging and labeling are extremely important. A knockout name for your dip, and a colorful folded tag, with artwork and several inviting recipes printed on it are surefire ways to merchandise dips. We have several delicious dips which we tout as "salt-free/sugar-free seasonings" for use as dips with chips and crudités as well. To illustrate their versatilities, we include tested recipes for soups, salads, veggies, and meat dishes on the folded tag. We also encourage our customers to share their tips and recipes with us (we give them a small gift in return) and include these on later tag printings. Of course, we always serve our dips at our in-store parties — with a basketful of the dip packages near by. It's a proven point of sales.

16 **Herb Garden Seasoning Mixtures** will rank up there with potpourri as a money maker. With the harvest from your garden, you can create endless seasoning combinations. They are easy enough to devise by combining the herbs from a favorite recipe and developing it into your private-label herb mix. Be sure to taste test it — family and friends will enjoy the task. Even customers can be pressed into service to help devise and approve a new seasoning. Take parsley, sage, rosemary, and thyme, for example, and formulate your seasoning thus: ten parts dried parsley, one part sage, two parts rosemary, three parts thyme. Mix thoroughly then distribute small amounts for critical sampling and suggested recipes. When you are satisfied, proudly print a label and you are on your way to success. Be *sure* to keep it all herbal and label it boldly "Salt-Free." There is a growing market of people on restricted diets, who view salt as a forbidden, four-letter word. Those customers who want it can always add salt.

There is a small herb shop near the seashore with its own savory seafood seasoning. They package their specialty in clean clamshells wrapped tightly in clear plastic. These attractive little souvenir packets are impossible to keep in stock.

17 **Devise a Bean Soup Mix** — a simple but popular idea that has helped pay off mortgages on firehalls and churches — and set it above the ordinary by including a packet of dried bean herbs. Summer savory is an absolute must, but you can also include a bit of chili powder, a whole bay leaf, some dried onion and garlic, parsley in quantity, and a pinch of oregano. Whether packaged in a sturdy baggie or an old-fashioned clear canning jar, the mixture of six, ten, or even a hearty fifteen dried beans is pretty to behold. Tie the herbs on in another baggie along with your recipe and you can count on repeat sales.

18 **Catnip** is a mainstay. Fresh or dried, seeds or plants, all those cat lovers out there are buying pussy's herb in all forms. My cat craves it to such an extent that catnip wreaths must be hung in the cellarway, and tussie mussies with catnip are only safe in the refrigerator. Catnip toys — fish, mice or nondescript forms — are a must for any true herb shop. We once had a retired milliner in Mechanicsburg who made the most exquisite catnip playthings from her attic of scrap fabrics. Velvets, satins, chintz, and plush were converted into tiny works of feline art, set with ribbons and roses. We provided pounds of dry catnip for her products, and were happy to pay for the finished toys. We also sell catnip tea packaged in baggies with bows.

19 **Seeds** are lucrative as small packets yield good prices. You can harvest some seeds that are a natural by-product of your herb garden. Those not usually found on the open market are especially valuable, such as hardy indigo, old-fashioned single hollyhock, and santolina. We also grow, gather, package, and sell seeds such as angelica and sweet cicely, which are only viable when fresh. Since many of our herbs are harvested before seeds are set, we also purchase seeds by the ounce or pound for resale. One liability to growing one's own seeds is that it means keeping the plant past its prime, making the garden look, well — seedy. In our small garden, neatness counts

for a lot, which means we must be selective as to what we allow to go to seed. Packaging seeds is one of my favorite tasks, and a good thing too. I learned early on that those who don't grow plants for seed think the goal is to get rid of them quickly. I parcel my seed out judiciously in very small packets knowing our supply is limited, and no one short of a commercial grower requires four hundred sage seeds.

Herb plants in pots can be sold right from your porch.

20 **Herbs in Small Pots** are whisked off our porch at a breathtaking pace. Between the vernal equinox and the autumnal equinox, we sell thousands of herb plants. In the spring, when gardening juices are flowing, we have flats of plants wall to wall, and the little plants virtually fly out of the garden. As long as they are self-contained in pots, the plants can be transplanted safely all summer long. Even a very small garden is a great source of rooted cuttings, divisions, or unwanted seedlings: pot them, label them, sell them. Everything sells!

Since we have a city garden on a tiny piece of land, we can't possibly grow all that we can sell. We are dependent upon wholesale growers and have many suppliers, some close at hand, others outside the state who supply us by mail order. We are constantly searching for unusual herbs for ourselves as well as our customers. We feel the expense of purchasing herb plants for resale is money well spent because we save the costs of building and heating greenhouses and employing all the help required to maintain such an operation. By combining the inventory from many available sources, we are able to offer a tremendous variety, a point of pride for us. We complement our outside sources by growing certain rare herbs ourselves — from seeds or from cuttings. But with our limited facilities, we restrict this to unusual herbs that we can't purchase elsewhere. We also buy from local gardeners who have surplus seedlings or comfrey roots they are willing to put in pots. We like to encourage the entrepreneurial spirit when we encounter it. Our best sellers? Parsley, of course. And dill and chives, too, the basics. But the top of the list is — are you ready for this? — mint! Yes, the one people rip out because it invades space given to other herbs is the one we sell the most of. We have as many varieties as we can find and sell every one. My message is loud and clear, turn your herb plants into profit! To triple your sale of plants, take a tip from master grower Sal Gilbertie, who suggests staging herbs alphabetically from anise to zebrovska.

21 **Grow Kits** are one of the fun things that you can package to encourage herb growing. Fill a bowed baggie with a few peat pellets, a pack of familiar herb seeds, a label, and an instruction sheet explaining the steps to germination success. We make wooden labels using a waterproof pen, assembly line all the ingredients, then stuff the baggies (which can be reused as part of the kit to encourage sprouting). Offer grow kits as special-order products — for quantity purchases of inexpensive, attractive favors.

22 **All Types of Kits** can be packaged (or you can hire home-based workers to package them for you). People love kits that hold everything neeeded for an easy craft. They buy them for themselves or as gifts for crafters, children, and people who can't get out to shop. All our kits contain everything needed except scissors or glue, along with detailed easy-to-follow instructions. We manufacture dried tussie-mussie kits, do-it-yourself potpourri kits, pomander kits (all but the orange), grow kits, pressed flower notepaper kits, "Have Fun Growing Herbs" kits (a herb gardening booklet by that name along with four seed packets), and Moravian star kits (an area craft). You might also try kits for herbal papermaking, a dried-flower brooch or barrette, a kitchen spice posey, and pinecone tree ornaments. We develop kits of the projects taught in our make-it-and-take-it workshops; these sell well to those who can't take the class or participants who wish to make another wreath, garland, swag, or whatever the project is. We know a craft shop whose mainstay business is small kits for summer camps and bible schools. They sell thousands: no employee is ever idle! Take heed, all you crafters.

23 **Wedding Potpourri** is one of the special products we developed for wedding celebrations by combining with rice or birdseed that is dyed in the bride's wedding colors. The dye is simply vegetable coloring, which rice or birdseed absorbs quickly. Once this combination is dried, we add roses for love, rosemary for remembrance, and a host of other symbolic wedding herbs. It can be sold by the pound for mass distribution, by the cupful as shower favors, or done up in individual four-inch net squares to match the bridal party. This was our first Rosemary House product, developed in June 1968, and it is still going strong. We have since developed attractive labels describing the symbolism of the ingredients in this popular wedding item.

24 **Stuffed Animals** have gained enormous appeal. They're not just for kids anymore. Stuffed with fragrant herbs, they are especially popular as an adult trophy. You can stitch your own, have them sewn for your shop, or find an inexpensive source of bunnies, bears, and dolls that can be opened and restuffed. Once filled with fragrant herbs or potpourri, these aromatic toys can be decorated for special occasions and holidays. My favorite is an Easter decoration, a floppy-eared bunny wearing glasses and stuffed with lavender. Sell them with small vials of oil to refresh the scent.

25 **Garden Accoutrements** fit right in your line. With the herb garden as your touchstone, bee skeps, bird feeders, wind chimes, sundials, concrete figurines, statuary and troughs, large containers, and even garden furniture are all possible additions to your inventory. For container gardeners, tubs and large pots are especially popular. Filled with herbs, these containers make a great accent for lawn, garden, patio, or deck. Whether you make your own concrete troughs or buy them for resale, consider carrying them. Antique garden furnishings are also much sought after, especially watering cans.

26 **"Lavender, Sweet Lavender,** Who will buy my lavender?" In Australia there is a herb cottage devoted entirely to lavender products: oils and perfume, soap and body lotion, sweet water for linens, moth repellents, potpourris and sachets, insect repellent, furniture polish, foot bath, night creams and talcum powder, incense, bath bags, lavender wands, baskets and wreaths, stuffed dolls and mice, candles, drawer liners, even a fragrant tea cozy and fans for a hot summer's day. That's not to overlook the culinary products: lavender flower conserve, teas, fritters, jellies, honey, biscuits, mustard, vinegar, and cake with lavender icing. For medicinal purposes, the cottage purveys lavender for headaches, as an

effective antiseptic wash, and as an ingredient in the famous "Hungary Water" beauty lotion, sleep pillows, inhalants, ointments, massage oil, and all the aromatherapy products. Need I say more?

27 **Herbal Topiaries** are the most endearing of all potted plants. They have taken the gardening world by storm! A $10 bay or rosemary is quickly elevated to a $20 product if you know how to prune lower leaves and branches so that you end up with the lollipop look. Other standards for topiaries are lemon verbena, upright thyme, scented geraniums, and true myrtle. If you don't grow your own, buy them for resale. Customers find herbal topiaries irresistible.

28 **Ordinary Baskets Filled with Herbs** become extraordinary. Line them with foil, fill with wetted floral foam, and stuff with assorted herbs and colorful flowers from your garden. These baskets make pretty, fragrant gifts, especially nice for nursing homes and hospitals. Cut everything the same length to assure an evenly rounded, symmetrical bouquet. Adding a bow is a nice touch.

29 **Dried Herbs.** If the basket bouquet described above withers before it is sold, rest assured it has served you well — by giving your shop a fresh herbal look. Moreover, you can recycle the arrangement by adding to it other dried flowers and fragrant herbs. Lavender, rosebuds, marjoram, mint, and others are just as pretty dried as fresh.

Learn to make fresh herbal topiaries (such as this geranium one) and you have a profitable product.

30 **Decorative Baskets** can be easy with a glue gun, bits of moss (Spanish or sheet), and dried flower heads. Glue the moss along the basket's rim, then bed down the moss with flowers and herbs until you achieve a colorful circlet. We use this method to recycle damaged baskets; it is also a great project for an easy, appealing workshop. Sometimes we cover the entire basket in moss and call it a fairy basket.

31 **Turn Garden Flowers into Lovely Works of Art.** Fresh flower arrangements with pretty, fragrant herbs are a natural, attractive addition to your shop's offerings and I urge you to develop the necessary skills. Although herbs lend themselves to naturalistic bouquets and bunches, a quick course in floristry will hone your skills at arranging herbs and flowers for special occasions. We profitably recycle a lot of unusual containers and nice baskets this way. You might consider adding a line of useful floral arranging equipment as well, such as containers, floral foam, water picks, all-purpose shears, corsage tape, and wire. Since we use these items ourselves, we order enough to stock for resale. A corner full of such items will help lure garden club ladies and others who like to do their own flower arranging into your shop.

32 **Dried Flowers** are the perfect complement to herbs. With a good supply of dried herbs and beautiful dried materials on hand, fresh-looking nosegays and other colorful crafts can be produced year-round. Since we don't have the land necessary to grow strawflowers and the other pretty drieds, we buy most of them for resale. There are many good commercial growers who wholesale their colorful product. Grow or buy them to use yourself and to sell, by the bunch or stem. We also sell craft bags of "dead heads" (loose flowers off the stem) by the ounce.

33 **Don't overlook the brisk market in wreaths, swags, and wall hangings** which depend upon dried flowers for color and herbs for fragrance. If you are not into crafts, go to craft fairs and seek out skilled artisans willing to supply your shop. These are high-ticket items. Many customers come in seeking these charming pieces of decor for their walls. I have visited homes with a wreath in every room.

Wreaths, swags, and wall hangings make a charming display in your shop and can sell for high prices.

I know one decorator who uses wreaths lavishly as her trademark. We also encourage special orders for different sizes, colors, or occasions. Wreath making not only produces consistent income, it is also my therapy.

34 **Nature Crafting** is a skill with endless possibilities, and one well worth developing. Along with wreaths, potpourris, and flower arranging (all mentioned in the preceding tips), other nature crafts ideas include: baskets made from vines; gourds cut and shaped into vases, pitchers, or birdhouses; Christmas ornaments made from twigs or pinecones; decorated hats; wheat weavings; shells and driftwood ornamented with herbs; seed or spice necklaces; cornhusk dollies; fungus pictures; herbal brooms; and a whole lot more. Harvesting whatever is free for the picking from your herb garden, nearby fields, roadside, and woodlands will reward you with bushels of beauty to bring indoors. Let the gatherings of herbs, flowers, twigs, cones, leaves, berries, and nuts guide your hands in creating a variety of natural crafts. Craft stores provide equipment, materials, direction books, and ideas for successful nature crafting. Consider using your projects as workshop offerings as well.

35 **The Rose** is a rose is a rose is a herb — to paraphrase a very familiar line. To some, the rose is the ultimate herb, useful in every way — entirely edible, fragrant, medicinal and cosmetic, ancient symbol of love, grown universally, beloved by all who grow it. All this and our national flower, too. There is nothing you can't create with the multifaceted rose — jams, jellies, vinegars, teas, sandwiches, perfumes, cold creams, crafts (fresh, dried, or pressed), sachets, potpourris, lotions and potions, and

The versatility of the rose makes it a herbal mainstay and a perfect complement to herbal crafts and bouquets.

decorations for weddings and holidays. The rose *is* a herbal mainstay. In our small garden, we have a shell pink tea rose ('Blossom Time') with perfect buds to use in the center of nosegays; a dark red climber ('Red Fountain') for vinegars; an old-fashioned *Rosa rugosa* with fragrant red flowers for potpourri and abundant orange-scarlet hips for teas; and nine pink polyanthas called 'The Fairy'. We can't grow enough of this perfect complement to all our herbal crafts and bouquets, fresh and dried. I'm sure the huge cotton candy trusses harbor fairies — they're such a charmer.

36 **Weeds** offer great potential as products. If you live near a field or have access to roadsides, you've got wild money there to be harvested. At one fall craft fair, we saw a parade of people carrying big bundles of weeds. Exploring the source, we found an enterprising garden club gathering weeds from nearby fields (with permission) in enormous sheaves, bunching and tying them on the spot — and filling their club coffers with ready cash! Honest! They were selling wild brown dock, goldenrod, white yarrow, fuzzy gray mullein, ferns, tan grasses mixed with colorful leaves, corn tops, wild oats, and whatever else was available. The farmers were glad to have their fields harvested, and customers happily purchased such reasonably priced decor for their city homes. I thought the busy ladies marvelously inventive. Include in this category bunches of twiggy branches, grapevine prunings, and bittersweet vines. Who says weeds are worthless? Think of them as wildflowers.

37 **Pressed Flower Pictures** are leaders in sales. People are charmed by colorful flowers and herbs captured artistically to decorate many kinds of things. While I enjoy this craft, The Rosemary House has several skilled artisans who gather, press, and create all manner of pressed crafts for resale. A few pressed herbs and flowers dress up a certificate, announcement, or wedding invitation to suit a queen. We do these as special orders by commissioning an artist. We also sell ornamented notecards and calligraphy in our regular line. I especially like to recycle useful items decorated with pressed materials. Barely used three-ring notebooks, wooden cigar boxes, and old barn wood are candidates for this art form. Unless it is under glass, the fragile beauties should be protected with a decoupage resin. You might also sell surplus pressed herbs and flowers to do-it-yourselfers, along with presses in various sizes.

38 **Fresh Tussie Mussies** from the herb garden are our most popular gift. Suitable for new mothers, honored persons, Secretary's Day, a 100th birthday, a bon voyage wish, proms, and wedding parties, these are, without exception, the loveliest tribute an herb garden can produce. We are justly proud of our tussie mussies. Fragrant, lovely, symbolic, and sentimental, we make them to order in all sizes — from silver-dollar-sized boutonnieres or favors to sizeable bride's bouquets. Prices vary greatly depending upon the size, time of year, and whether or not we need to purchase florist roses. Lace or paper collars and fluffy ribbons must be figured into the cost. However, it's the fragrant, charming, quiet herbs that are the most important component. Florists can't do these scent-imental nosegays. They are the most versatile of herbal bouquets.

39 **Colorful Dried Nosegays** are a great year-round product to have available right off the shelf, with no preordering necessary. You can make them by poking or gluing stemmed flowers into a floral foam holder, available from your wholesale florist (look for listings in the Yellow Pages). Add a lacy collar and ribbon streamers, and you have a pretty addition to your shop's inventory that will put cash in the drawer. To make the nosegays smell as good as they look, add a few drops of essential oil to each one.

40 **Herb Gardening Supplies,** bought at wholesale, or even retail, and broken up into smaller saleable amounts is a fair way to profit. Most people really don't need a hundred saffron bulbs, six cubic yards of potting soil, a hundred pounds of a special fertilizer, or a thousand pot labels. Use what you need for your shop or garden operation — then package what's left for resale. If they're priced right, properly labeled, and displayed attractively, these products will move.

41 **Medicinal Herbs** are experiencing a renewal, as people selling them are well aware. I was unprepared for and impressed by the rising demand. Our front door sign clearly states "Fragrances and Flavors," yet a large amount of our business is in botanicals and natural remedies. We have built a handsome corner area in our shop out of old barn wood to house all our traditional medicinals. They are displayed in gallon jars, labeled and priced so that people can purchase a half-ounce or a pound of anything that is legal. Our inventory, knowledge, and respect for medicinals have grown along with customer demand.

Customers buy herbal medicinals in all forms: fresh from the garden; dried in teas; as drops, skin butters, salves, balms, beauty aids, herbal shampoos, and natural hair dyes; in capsules, lotions, gentle baby products, and diet aids; and whatever else you may stock. Don't overlook this enormously profitable market.

We buy most of our medicinal products from professionals who use FDA-approved labeling and have health-department-approved manufacturing areas. When you enter the business of herbs, be assured that you will find yourself drawn into this fascinating market. Before you begin, be sure that you are aware of federal regulations in this area (*see* pages 133 – 34). Even if you should decide not to tap into this market, you should be informed about the medicinal properties of herbs.

> *"In my youth," said the Sage, as he shook his grey locks, "I kept all my limbs very supple By the use of this ointment — one shilling the box — Allow me to sell you a couple."*
> Lewis Carroll
> *Alice in Wonderland*

42 **Aloe** ranks up there with the most indestructible of houseplants. It is also an indispensable herb. Called "the burn plant," "the doctor plant," the "medicine plant," or properly *Aloe vera,* it is the number-one home remedy that can be grown on the windowsill, where it will tolerate considerable neglect. Aloe even grows with a northern light exposure, making it easy to display in your shop window. From my three large mother plants that have huge clumps spilling out of their tubs, I occasionally harvest a dozen offshoots and pot them up for quick resale. Since aloe is supported by a relatively small root, be careful never to plant any of the succulent leaves under the soil, where they could rot.

43 **Ancient Herbs** have galloped into the twentieth century, carried along by the Age of Aquarius, which has produced a different kind of herb business. While not for everyone, esoteric New Age herb shops inspire great loyalty among their customers. Herbs can

become the catalyst for a shop offering crystals, incense, candles, and aromatherapy. With meditative music playing in the background, modern and ancient inspirational books, techniques, and materials are purveyed along with essential oils, all the Edgar Cayce remedies, tapes, natural foods, and healing workshops. Herbs, fresh or dried, are right at home here, lending both fragrance and mystery to the atmosphere. The New Age shop is a whole other dimension of the business of herbs.

44 **Cultivate your Artist Connections!** An artist who can transfer the charms of growing herb plants onto paper or canvas is a valuable source for new products and presentations. We are constantly on the lookout for talent — and press our artist friends into service as often as we can afford another commission. Sometimes we discover hidden talent in our own mail. When we receive an order or letter with distinctive handwriting, we ask the writer to design a Rosemary House label. Sometimes we swap merchandise for artwork. Once the work is designed we select paper and colors, obtain estimates from several printers and — voila! — a new herb chart, poster, product label, or notepaper is on our shelves. A word of caution: Unless you are your own artist, never hurry the creative spirit. A deadline is helpful, but don't count on it. Artists, bless them all (we couldn't operate without them), march to their own drummer.

45 **Writing!** This could be the ultimate harvest from your herb garden — sometimes it's even profitable. I enjoy writing and entertain a vast correspondence. Given idle time, I find myself with pen in hand. I often regret not setting down on paper my learning experiences from when I first got interested in herbs, when everything in and out of the herb garden was new and wonderful. It's still wonderful, but the excitement and awe of discovery — the magic that grows in a brand-new herb garden — must now be recaptured from the deep wellspring of my heart and head. At the time, feeling a novice, I didn't realize I should have been writing down every observation. What was new and wonderful to me then would have been just as new and wonderful to others. Eventually I began writing a weekly column for our local paper. These articles are still good today, and I use them as handy reference. If you have a penchant for writing, share your herb discoveries with others through publication in newspapers and newsletters. This is superb publicity for your shop, as well as additional income. Write on!

46 **Recipes** are your secret weapon. Every recipe you have tried and altered, every recipe you have devised and served, is your herb shop's asset. We print our recipes on our labels to encourage use of our products, we post them on our bulletin board, print them separately for distribution, offer them as favors at open houses, luncheons, or tea parties, and freely share and swap herbal recipes with our customers. Even the most creative cook, who already has an entire library of cookbooks, will pick up our special shop recipes. Most people are interested in cooking — or at least in eating — and will keep recipes. So we print them on almost any notice along with our name and address. Never underestimate the power of a recipe. When you have developed and tested enough, put them all together for your very own shop cookbook — another product to sell!

> *When you are near a plant and in its aura, as when you are under a tree, for instance, you are fed its radiations. When you eat of the plant, you are fed its radiations on another level of your being. One method can be as important as the other. This is another reason for spending time in the garden.*
> From *The Findhorn Story* by The Findhorn Community

47 **Newsletters.** There's so much to be said — and written — about herbs that you may soon have a newsletter if you aren't careful. I have toyed with developing one, but the prospect of selling subscriptions, mounting ads, and seeking contributors threatens to take too much from the time, energy, and fun I want to devote to The Rosemary House. Deadline phobia — realizing a newsletter needs to be written and distributed regularly — is my greatest deterrent. But if deadlines don't bother you, then go for it. The field is wide open, and the material is inexhaustible. Moreover, you will have an open forum for your shop advertising herb gardens, products, workshops, and special events. Bear in mind that writing is a stern taskmaster, not for everyone. To be successful, you need to write every day, even if it's just checks.

48 **Books** unlock the secrets of herbs and deserve primary consideration for your inventory. You will find that books outsell anything else in your shop. Rank beginner, inquiring novice, skilled herbalist, cook, gardener, history buff, crafts person — all sorts of people will peruse your bookshelves, for all sorts of reasons. Customers who enter The

Rosemary House out of curiosity almost always gravitate toward our book section and usually purchase one.

Take one look at the extensive herbal library covering my walls, and you'll see that books can easily become an addiction. Everyone has questions — don't you? — and the answers can be found in books, old and new. The history and ancient usage of herbs in all the cultures and civilizations

Antiques complement a herb business perfectly, adding display areas and additional income if sold.

of the world have been ferreted out and put down on paper. The mysteries, the magic, and the depths of these "plants with a purpose" were written in stone millennia ago — let us plumb the depths! Dollars invested in book inventory will yield both knowledge and profits. We sell so many books that our accountant lists our product line as "Herbs/Books."

49 Antiques go hand in hand with herbs — but the herbs are older! If you are an antique lover and have a large collection, your shop serves you in two ways. First, you can use many prize pieces as decor to dress your displays and, second, you have a chance to sell off surplus bits of your burgeoning collection. Every antique we put up for sale in our shop found an eager buyer quickly, especially duplicates of old herbals. We see these antique sales as chances to recover our investment, as well as to upgrade the pieces in our private collection. Many herb shops are located in old buildings that lend charm to the country look of antiques. Our old drugstore cabinets are showpieces. We also scatter old bean crocks and other pottery pieces stuffed with bunches of herbs and weeds throughout the shop. It's a profitable way to recycle your flea market and yard sale finds. Old herbal medicine bottles with interesting labels and spice tins are comfortable additions. We have sold a host of apothecary jars both new and old. Hundreds of old blue canning jars with zinc lids have passed through our hands — some empty and some filled with cinnamon sticks, dried parsley, or potpourri. We have also sold many antique reproductions made by local craftspeople including wooden spice cupboards, handmade tin cookie cutters, and springerle molds, but we always mark them honestly. Likewise, we know several antique dealers who have added herbs to their shops. Starting in a small corner of the shop, the herbs have nestled in and become a growing presence in response to customer demand, while adding fragrance, spewing ambience, and increasing profits for the antique dealer as well.

50 **Dried Stems** contain as much or more aromatic oils as the more popular leaves and flowers — so don't throw a bit of your precious herbal harvest away. After you make your wreaths or potpourris, tie up leftover bunches of stems, and add a few pretty drieds as an extra touch. Using colorful ribbon or utilitarian twine, affix an explanatory label — "To start a fragrant fire" — and put a price on your scrap bundles.

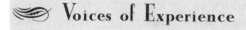

Voices of Experience

CELLAR BABIES BY JOHANNA'S
JoANNE FAJACK

Housewife, mother, and now grandmother, JoAnne Fajack has always loved herbs. She cooks with them, decorates with them, and uses them in all her arrangements. But she especially uses them in her handmade, one-of-a-kind doll.

JoAnne gave up a career teaching school to study floral design. Using her background as an art teacher along with her newfound design knowledge, she designed and stitched her Cellar Babies, her own trademarked product. These clever antique-looking, tea-dyed herbal dolls come in all sizes and carry baskets, bouquets, or wreaths of herbs and spices. Each one is given a name and his or her own winsome personality. All the herbs come from JoAnne's three gardens.

Now sold in half a dozen shops, Cellar Babies are also exhibited at large juried craft shows, where JoAnne gets an enthusiastic response from both doll collectors and herb enthusiasts.

COUNTRY PETALS HERBAL POTTERY
SHARON MAGEE

One of Sharon Magee's friends gave her a mint plant, and she discovered the joys of potpourri making — pounds of it, given to family and friends. When Sharon Magee realized she had run out of people to give it to, she either had to make more friends or start selling it.

In a year's time she had eight different blends of potpourri and eight craft shows under contract. Her Country Petals business had begun. Reading all she could find about herbs, especially crafting them, Sharon soon added potpourri ornaments, potpourri dolls, lavender wands, spice ropes and mats, herb pillows, and dried arrangements to an endless list of clever fragrant items.

After ten years of packing and unpacking for craft sales, Sharon wearied of this. That's when she put up a small building on her property in Aberdeen, Maryland and let the customers come to her.

Sharon fell upon a new product idea when she began looking for herb markers for her garden. Not finding them elsewhere, the intrepid craftsperson turned to clay to make them herself. When she discovered the charming imprints herbs made in clay, she fell in love all over again.

With a sales philosophy of "don't do what everyone else does — make it unique," Sharon left the world of potpourris. Pottery decorated with herb imprints has become her main product line — herb markers, pins, personalized and dated plaques celebrating life's special occasions, bowls, plates, serving dishes, and wind chimes are all among her products. Both retail and wholesale, Sharon's shop is open by appointment only. Although she works full-time for the government, she considers herbs her full-time life.

BRIER ROSE HERBS
MARK AND ROSE BURAS

"Herb gardening in the Deep South can be frustrating, to say the least," writes Rose Buras of Brier Rose Herbs, based in Belle Chase, Louisiana. With limited information available,

Rose has started a one-page newsletter to answer the hundreds of questions she is asked.

Her first business enterprise began as a horticulture program for retarded citizens. Growing herbs for the fresh-cut market in New Orleans, the program proved so successful they were able to pay the handicapped employees real wages.

When she moved to Belle Chase, Rose started her own business growing and marketing four-inch potted herbs to garden centers and nurseries in the New Orleans area. Begun in her backyard, the enterprise quickly spread to a friendly neighbor's backyard and next door to her in-laws. To ease the growing pains of their new venture, she and her husband plan to purchase four acres of land.

Because she has learned the special care required by herbs in the Deep South, Rose has plans to turn her informative monthly newsletter into a book devoted to accurately portraying the difficult growing conditions for herbs in the New Orleans area. She is conducting trial plantings, using a diary to record results, and collecting shared gardening experiences from her readers.

PRIME AREAS FOR EXPANDING YOUR PRODUCTS

TRADITIONAL MEDICINES

As herb professionals, don't ever put down the role of herbs in health. Even though it may not be part of your personal philosophy, in centuries gone by "simples" such as sage tea and mustard plasters were standard procedures. They work as well today as they ever did in the hands of those who know how to use them.

With the rising costs of modern medical care, we all need to understand alternative treatments such as acupuncture, homeopathy, stress control, biofeedback, and the basic healing properties of herbs. I'm not for a minute suggesting we encourage self-diagnosis or treatment. But on the other hand, we are fools to ignore home remedies and herbal help that has worked effectively for ages. Remember that the first use of herbs was in medicines, and that today's pharmacopoeia utilizes plants in over 50 percent of its prescriptions. Customers are intent on taking control and being responsible for their health and bodies.

Libraries of books on the subject are available. We stock and sell a great many herbals, old and new. We are also fascinated by true stories of better health through herbs which our customers gladly share with us. We keep a file of herbal treatments some have found effective. We also maintain an up-to-date address book of naturopaths, homeopaths, and even a veterinarian who treats animals with herbs.

A few physicians send patients to us for raspberry leaf tea (for pregnant ladies) or catnip and camomile (natural sedatives) or ginger capsules (for motion sickness). We also sell aloe plants all year long for their healing qualities that date back to biblical times.

Within the FDA's guidelines on labeling, you can sell your herbal harvest as home remedies that are both helpful and harmless. For instance, we sell pennyroyal, a delicious minty tea also useful as a flea repellent, with a red "caution" card warning that it can also be an abortant.

Write to the Federal Food and Drug Administration, 200 C Street, SW, Washington, DC 20204, and request their GRAS (Generally Recognized as Safe) list of herbs and plants. If you plan to manufacture and market cosmetics or herbal medicinals, you will also need to know their proper labeling requirements.

Don't even think of marketing an herbal drug or cosmetic until you have checked out all the FDA regulations and ramifications. If you go this route, you may wish to consult a lawyer. There are specialists in the field of labeling.

> *Herbs still have a useful place in coping with many of the ills to which mankind is heir. This is particularly true in the case of the so-called minor ailments of life such as indigestion, coughs, and pains. Inevitably, therefore, it is these minor ills which predominate. Minor, however, is something of a misnomer. What may be "minor" to the doctor may be anything but minor to the patient, for whom it may make life unbearable. Nature has many remedies for our ailments. Tested in many cases through the ages, these natural remedies still claim attention as herbs that heal.*
> William A.R. Thomson, M.D.,
> *Medicines from the Earth*

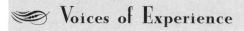

HEALING HEART HERBALS
CINDY PARKER

"To me," says Cindy Parker, "herbalism is not only a profession but a way of life." While on a work exchange program at the California School of Herbal Studies in 1978, Cindy, her husband, and two-month-old son were introduced to their lifetime study: traditional medicinals.

Cindy took this newfound knowledge back to their home in Ohio where she and her mother opened a little herb shop and Cindy taught classes. Several household moves, unplanned side roads, and three children later, Cindy has settled into Healing Heart Herbals. Since opening in 1987, Cindy has offered classes, workshops, yearly herbal retreats, and an annual health fair. She also sponsors six-month herbal apprenticeship programs and a herb school, open from April through September.

Healing Heart Herbals' product line includes many natural herbal products for pleasure and healing. Cindy makes and sells her own bath oils, bath bags, bath salts, Barefoot Pleasures foot oil, Aphrodite love oil, and, a favorite, Hippy Turtle bath oil. Ma Parker's Healing Heart Herbal booklets teach customers and students how to make their own herbal preparations.

Cindy markets these booklets and products through private in-home parties and in popular, practical customized gift baskets: bath baskets, love baskets, foot baskets, first aid baskets, kid's baskets — anything the customer wants.

Most of all, Cindy enjoys lecturing and teaching the subject she loves and knows so well. With a crusader's zeal, she wants to inspire others to take responsibility and be active participants in achieving their own health and well-being, and to increase their awareness of the many remarkable aspects of herbs.

INDOOR HERB GARDENING

A herb shop needs herbs, it's as simple as that. Even a city store with no windows can brighten a dark corner with a display of a few herbs in pots — with today's fluorescent grow light systems you can grow herbs even in a closet!

For many years, with the approach of January and the winter doldrums, we whisked clean a back-room area and set up an old galvanized tray under a four-foot light stand. The tray was filled with white pebbles and water to provide humidity in a hot, dry shop, as well as essential drainage for the herbs.

Under the light, we grew pots of parsley, sage, rosemary, and thyme, along with seedlings elevated close to the light on inverted pots. Even though we have a small greenhouse, this splash of light and green tucked in amidst the merchandise proved an eye-catching display, a fun activity, and a practical way to grow herbs indoors in wintertime. Herb plants in pots are moveable and saleable as well as decorative and useful.

Grow light units are available in a variety of styles and sizes from carts, some as tall as six tiers, to compact units as small as a reading lamp. They can also be built to suit any available space. There is great flexibility in the ways you can bring the freshness and charm of herbs indoors. Don't feel restricted until you have explored all that's available from your nearest nursery center or through the mail.

Growing herb plants under lights in your shop brings the freshness of herbs indoors and offers an opportunity to display and sell related goods.

There are many useful items on the market for indoor growing. Although we invested in lights specially designed for plant growth, we have also used discarded fluorescent lamps from garages, with little significant difference in plant growth. Incandescent light is not advisable because of the heat and danger of leaf burn.

Because herbs require more hours of light daily than the shop hours, we invested in a timer that turns the grow lights on automatically at 7 A.M. and off at 7 P.M. We have gone so far as to indulge in a small hydroponic set-up — with exciting results. To my amazement, even chives thrived. (I expected their little bulbs would rot in the constant moisture.) We enjoyed many cuttings from these extremely productive plants.

Some herbs — sage, thyme, and lavender for instance — that have never done well as houseplants on our sunniest windowsill responded beautifully to grow light culture. What fun to keep a little scissors handy and snip tiny, fragrant nosegays, to the surprise of our visitors.

In-shop gardening under lights offers lots of related resale opportunities too. You can start seeds and root cuttings for sale and display; offer equipment for misting, fertilizing, and grooming nearby; and herb seeds will definitely sell readily near a display of growing plants. You will boost sales of all the wintertime items for growing plants indoors when you offer customers an exciting display of herbs growing under lights. And you'll have fun doing it.

Excellent herbs
had our fathers of old,
Excellent herbs
to ease their pain,
Alexanders and marigold,
Eyebright, orris
and elecampane.
Rudyard Kipling

A TISKET A TASKET, A LITTLE YELLOW BASKET

Baskets aren't just for Easter anymore. At least 20 percent of our gift business is done in baskets. Since the beginning of The Rosemary House, we have encouraged customers to select or allow us to put together a customized basket of herbal goodies for that special person on that special occasion. We call them Baskets of Love.

Fragrances, flavors, teas, and gardening supplies are only a few of the specialties we can assemble in a basket from our vast stock of small, useful items. Just tell us it's a seventy-fifth birthday gift for Aunt Sarah who has a cat, doesn't do much cooking, plays bridge with a large circle of friends, and loves purple — and we will happily work up a pretty basketful that is guaranteed to delight her. We'll top the basket off with a fragrant tussie mussie caught in lavender ribbons, of course.

For a twenty-fifth anniversary we have silver foil; for a country look we recycle excelsior. For Victoriana lovers, we'll use a snowy white crocheted doily as a liner. At holiday times — Easter, Valentine's Day, Mother's Day, and especially Christmas — our nimble-fingered basket makers are tying bows day and night to keep ahead of the demand. These versatile gifts are the brilliant solution to finding a gift for everyone on a long list. We also whip up tiny baskets in quantity for favors at a large party or convention.

Baskets can be tailored to any occasion, as well as to any budget. We love doing the $100 ones but we will do a $10 one just as cheerfully. For the latter, we use ordinary strawberry baskets so that the dollars can be stretched a bit. Most of our baskets fall in the $20 to $30 range.

In place of wicker, we also like to start with a large, flat cookbook or tray and assemble a tiered look by stacking boxed items on it. Building layers on a sturdy base is easier than a basket and, topped by a huge bow, can be showier, too.

Baskets made-to-order according to the recipient's interests can become a profitable mainstay of your business.

Hand-decorated clay pots, wire egg baskets, quiche pans, woks, mortar and pestles, and mugs are all excellent receptacles for gift items. Almost anything is possible, and if it's unique, all the better. We have done baskets for a bachelor's birthday, kitchen showers, a new mother (a fragrant bath basket), a new homeowner (a gardening basket), a teenager (soaps and sachets), a dedicated cook (seasonings and recipes), and many more.

We have several real estate salespeople who crown their sales with a gift basket from The Rosemary House. One of them tells us that most of her clients use the basket as a centerpiece in place of flowers, admiring it until the bows wilt. These baskets are a joy to put together because we know they are well received, and chances are good that the newcomer will eventually seek out our shop.

Our wedding baskets are bountiful bouquets of tissue, lace, and white ribbons galore. These spectacular baskets are particularly appropriate for office gifts when a group has collected $78.94 or some such odd amount; we can adjust the contents accordingly. Moreover, once the gang sees the extravagant presentation of their gift, other orders will roll in. We had one boss's wife who admired the basket purchased for an employee and requested one for her own Christmas present.

All of our employees are taught basket selection along with bow making. Bows make the basket happen! They lend support, pull it all together, and top it off gloriously in any color scheme desired. Even those customers who choose to fill a decorative bag with choice items appreciate a bow on top.

Increase your sales by offering to mail your gifts. With this easy-care shopping service, you can take an order over the phone, write the gift card, and mail it off promptly. Don't include vinegars or bath oils, and be sure to make everything secure so that the recipient receives a perfect basket with unruffled bows. A service of this caliber deserves all the promotion you can give it.

Because we are justifiably proud of our herbal gift baskets, we never ever use outdated or distressed merchandise. Nor do we stuff a large container with excessive padding to camouflage how few items are in it. And all our baskets are lavishly hand bowed for that knock-out impact.

Clay pots, mugs, and books make unusual foundations for gift packages.

We usually top our creations with a bunch of herbs or dried flowers along with a baggie of something special tied up in the fluffy bow. Free gift cards are the finishing touch.

 ## Voices of Experience

WHAT CHEER HERBS
JANET AND JOHN BALLETTO

Janet and John Balletto have found a niche selling specialty herbal gift baskets. They run a busy mail-order and craft-show business while both work full-time jobs.

Their first herbal gift basket was devised especially for a new mother and first baby. To make the gift unique, they concocted Nursing Mother Tea, Baby Diaper Rash Salve, and a selection of other useful fundamental delights. In the meantime, word of mouth brought other customers their way, and soon Janet and John had a reputation as the "herbal gift basket people."

A successful craft fair added impetus to the budding business. More and more people wanted the cute, practical baskets. Three years after the first basket, the Ballettos' shoestring enterprise is showing a profit.

As they continue working to perfect their packaging, labeling, and product presentation, the Ballettos move closer to achieving their dream — to open a full-time shop for What Cheer Herbs.

Co-Op Consignments

Selling handmade goods on consignment is a good way to expand your inventory, bring in some extra cash, and support your local artisans. Because we pride ourselves on being important to the community and the lives of many in addition to our customers, The Rosemary House encourages consignment merchandise. Many skilled craftspeople and artists, seeking to support themselves or provide supplemental income, bring us their herbal creations to sell. This joint marketing venture helps us both: the craftspeople are paid for their work, and we are paid a commission. It also provides us with a greater variety of interesting merchandise to dress up the shop and entice customers — merchandise that changes with the seasons, especially for Christmas. By agreement with the artisans, we pay only for what is sold. Initially we charged a very low 20 percent of the retail price for our service, but with inflation and the rising costs of doing business, our fee has increased to 40 percent. Sometimes we purchase outright those crafts that we know will sell quickly.

You should develop your own policy in regard to consignments. Keep in mind that most craftspeople must pay rent when they take their wares to a craft show. To merchandise entirely out of their homes takes advertising, which is equally expensive. Even then, they may have a limited audience and produce a meager income. Consignment shops provide a very valuable service for these people.

The only disadvantage of taking consignments is the book work. It requires doing monthly inventory and writing individual checks for each artisan — not my idea of fun. On the other hand, exciting crafts and the work of a well-known craftsperson lure more people into our shop.

We prefer to carry crafts that are herb-related. We ask the craftsperson to make an appointment to bring in their wares before we accept them. We insist that they set their own prices since we don't know their material costs or the production time involved. And who dares to set a price on talent?

There are craftspeople who want to sell their work, regardless of whether the price reflects the number of hours spent on the project or not. In the end, the buying public determines whether the price is fair.

Our consignors include a watercolorist, a potter, wreath makers, a weaver, a woodworker who makes flower presses, a pressed flower person who works on consignment to fill special orders, a candle maker, a pinecone wizard, a gentleman who makes soaps and vinegars, a basketmaker, a honey hobbiest, and a seamstress who stitches leftover fabrics into aprons or sachet bags. We never know who will come our way next.

The most unusual? A gifted social worker who scans the woods for bits of moss, twigs, pods, and fungus which she mounts into exquisite wall hangings. The most popular? A school teacher who skillfully designs notepapers and framed pictures containing pressed flowers and herbs. We can't keep her work in stock.

One word of advice for guiding your artisans. Impress upon them that herbs need to be identified. Hand-painted slates with utterly charming paintings didn't sell at all until we convinced the artist to label them "dill," "mint," "bergamot." When she realized that even parsley went unrecognized, she began to imbue her lovely herbs with notes on the ancient, deeper hidden virtues of herbs: "Parsley for Victory," "Lavender for Luck," "Roses for Love," "Rosemary for Remembrance," and "Camomile, Courage in Adversity." These appealing little slates conveyed a magical message, making the perfect gift, and selling beyond her wildest dreams.

Chapter 7

SPECIAL EVENTS AND SERVICES TO BOLSTER YOUR BUSINESS

WORKSHOPS AND CLASSES — THE WAY TO GO!

EVEN AS I WRITE, the mail carrier is delivering four thousand invitations to The Rosemary House workshops and special events for the year. We expect our phones to ring continuously for the following week or two as classes fill. If people haven't found your shop yet, entice them with some public workshops. And encourage your customers to give their friends workshop gift certificates for birthdays and holidays.

Workshops and classes are well worth adding to your busy schedule because they will make a name for your enterprise, increase sales, and help educate the public. Any way you can spread the word, introduce others to the mysteries of herbs, and advance your business is a viable avenue to explore.

You are not craft-minded? Then bring other people in to teach your workshops. Whether you have a dining room table that seats only six comfortably, or a spare room and chairs for forty, you can hold workshops that will introduce you and your shop to more people faster than any other way. And you stand to profit from the sales of materials before and after the session.

As I recommended for your herb lectures (see page 97), build on your strong points to plan workshops, lectures, demonstrations, or hands-on events. Whatever your interests — cooking, fragrances, symbolism, wreaths, pressed-flower crafts, weddings, basketry, herbal cosmetics, potpourri — the workshop possibilities are endless. Planning and planting a herb garden is our most popular workshop; we give it every year at least once, sometimes thrice.

We set up our workshop schedule months in advance so that people can work the dates into their plans and we have sufficient time to fill the classes. Most workshops are scheduled for three different times to accommodate a variety of schedules: once in the morning, repeated the next afternoon, and again the following evening. Since so many of our customers work during the day, evening classes usually fill first. We often open a second evening class or, for our most popular courses (like wreath making), we also schedule a Saturday morning class.

Our classes are set up in our workshop (otherwise known as the garage) where we can seat twenty for a lecture-demonstration or ten for a hands-on session. It is a perfect place to make messes since it is easily swept. We also store our supplies in the workshop and it doubles as a drying shed. We advise all attendees to dress casually and comfortably.

Our registration/refund/cancellation policy on workshops is strict. "Your check reserves your seat" is written on every schedule. We also say, "If cancellation occurs a week before the class and we have a waiting list, money is cheerfully refunded. Otherwise, if we can't fill the seat and you don't send a substitute, we will give you a kit to make the item or, if it's a demonstration, all the handouts." We are also willing to accommodate paid registrants in another workshop on a seating-available basis.

WORKSHOP TOPICS

Make-it-and-take-it workshops are definitely the most popular. People love to learn a new craft and finish a project without having to shop around for the dozens of supplies beforehand, or to clean up afterward. We offer a variety of such workshops, introducing a few new ones every year along with the "oldies but goodies." Some people take the same workshop annually, making a new wreath each time for their own home or to give as a gift.

Some workshop ideas to consider: swags, garlands, topiaries, potpourri, pressed or dried-flower pictures, pinecone work, natural cosmetics, tussie mussies, living herb wreaths for Advent, garden troughs, and herbal papermaking. But don't be limited by my ideas. You will expand your workshop listings depending on your skills or teachers you discover. We have a young male teacher who is an expert on vinegar making and herbal beverages, including wines. His popular classes, which are tasting parties as well as make-it-and-take-it, attract more men than our other workshops.

No doubt about it, our best-attended workshops are the Christmas herbal decorations and tree ornament ones, which we follow with an elaborate holiday high herb tea party. Participants sign up for these festive occasions year after year, and sometimes treat their friends to one as a special Christmas gift.

PRICING WORKSHOPS

Pricing workshops is a bit tricky. If you price them out of your market, people simply will not come. At the same time, you want to be sure to cover your costs. Don't overlook a thing in estimating costs. Be careful — don't cheat yourself! All necessary materials (glue, wire frames, ribbons, etc.) you purchase are an expense; even herbs, or pressed or dried flowers you get "free" from the garden need to be figured in at retail price. Then there's the teacher's fee, and overhead such as rent, heat, and light.

The amazing part about pricing a workshop is that a wreath sold off the wall in the shop for $25 may cost that much for workshop participants to make on their own. Although we sell handmade pressed flower notepapers for $2.50 each, the workshop can be the same price or more. Each participant makes five notes for a $15 fee. But, people are willing to pay that much for receiving instructions plus the inexpensive materials.

I maintain a working file on workshops. Every listing that comes my way from other sources, every good idea I garner from a lecture or book, every potential teacher in or out of the area I hear about goes in that file for future reference. It is a treasure trove that serves us well when we sit down to plan our workshop schedule.

Actually, we don't have enough time or energy to do it all. The potential topics for herbal workshops are beyond imagination — and the potential income from them is as great as anything you may make from what you grow for your shop.

BRING ON THE EXPERTS

Just because you don't know the answers to all the questions about herbs is no reason to keep your customers uninformed. Hire a well-known expert and sponsor a class, lecture, or workshop. As the sponsor, not the presenter, be a guest at your own party. We have sponsored events that required us to rent the closest church social hall to accommodate the crowd, providing plenty of tables for the workshop, a large kitchen to serve lunch, and adequate parking. And so many wanted to hear our expert that we still had to schedule another workshop!

Our experts have included a marvelous perfume maker, well-known cookbook authors who offer lecture-demonstrations, a knowledgeable naturopath who taught us a great deal about herbal medicines, a flower arranger who designs with herbs, a craftperson/author with a host of clever ideas, and well-known herbalists from other areas. Given a lead about a possible superstar, we pursue it relentlessly.

In order to make an event like this work, you must do extensive advance publicity and take care of all the details such as handling registration and fees, hosting your guest of honor, and cleaning the site, especially if it is off your premises.

We don't believe in keeping public events a secret, especially when we realize how much they do for The Rosemary House as well as the world of herbs in general. These experts are always important people, and we don't want to risk failure. We send out press releases, print up posters and flyers, and make public announcements wherever we go. In addition to sending notices to our usual workshop mailing list, we have been known to send personal invitations to those on our Christmas card mailing list.

An outstanding personality almost guarantees you free notices, and sometimes even articles and interviews with newspapers, radio, and television. Send your press releases to national magazines as well as to your local newspapers and radio and television stations. We have had registrants come from other states, near and far.

Be sure to charge an enrollment fee that covers the advertising costs as well as rent, materials, and all your speaker's expenses and fees. We usually add up all our anticipated costs and divide by twenty, the lowest number of attendees we expect, thus arriving at a fee. After that, we work like the dickens to register those first twenty people. Anything we make beyond the basic costs allows us to offer printed handouts, perhaps a door prize, and to bank a nice profit for the shop for our work.

Sometimes there is no fee for hiring the expert, especially if he or she has recently written a new book. In such cases, we are more than willing to arrange a book signing, for which we serve tea and other herbal goodies at the shop. The books are usually available on consignment, so the ones we don't sell are returnable. Again, well-planned publicity is the key to the success of such an event.

Although sponsoring an expert speaker may prove to be more work than mounting your own workshops, you will soon discover that your business will be handsomely rewarded for your efforts, with fame and, perhaps, fortune.

HERB FESTIVALS

Are you ready for this? You have initiated your herbal business and herb people are seeking you out. Moreover, you have a nice-sized area around your shop including lots of room for parking — a great place to stage a fair!

Now that you have attracted a network of kindred spirits eager to join the fun, think "Herb Fair." A herb fair can be the highlight of your year, an event to put your business squarely on the map. Organization is the key to mounting a fair. Cooperation is also way up there on the list; you will need a good deal of help. High energy, stamina, and good weather belong there, too. This project is not for the timid or uninspired. On the other hand, it is an ultimate achievement and can make a lot of people happy. Just don't overlook publicity and you'll be successful. *Herbs* is a magic word. I personally prefer a herb fair that is entirely herb- and garden-related. There are many arts and crafts fairs, which are fun to stroll, but a herb fair promises herbs and should deliver on that promise. Make it a specific requirement. It's quite amazing what falls within that category.

Setting a date for the herb fair a year in advance is not too soon. You will need a year to develop all your ideas, arrange contracts with vendors, speakers, the food concessionaire, and parking attendants, and do publicity.

Enlist the aid of your network of friends as vendors or speakers, or both. Invite them to a committee meeting or two to contribute ideas, then send them home with handouts for their friends, neighbors, family, and customers. The more ideas you assemble, the better your event will be, and the more volunteers you recruit early on, the easier it will be to carry out your ideas.

Check out local rules on zoning. Town officials love to enforce regulations — and you don't need any surprises. Call the police or the town office, or whoever you think should be informed. Be sure to cover them all! This is also a good chance to invite your leading town or city official to cut the ribbon to open the fair.

One of the big decisions you'll have to make is what to charge. You will have expenses and will want your herb fair to be self-sustaining, perhaps even to turn a profit. Will you charge an entrance fee? A parking fee? A vendor's fee? Who makes the food and who makes the money from the food? These are crucial decisions and need to be made early.

Speakers, displays, or demonstrations on the many aspects of herbs will increase your fair's drawing power. Seek out experts in the field who are willing to share their expertise. Then publicize who will be doing what, when. Be specific — and then be sure your presenters are prompt, since people will come just for special features such as these. Sometimes the speakers will wave their fees in return for publicity and a free sales table. Negotiate all this well beforehand, and be sure to put it down on paper. If you make money, pay them. It's only fair.

Fair signage is an important part of your publicity as well. Each vendor and speaker deserves a sign, as well as a name and address listing in your herb fair program. This program can be a one sheet flyer, or a souvenir booklet in which you sell additional advertising. If the program is sprinkled with useful herbal hints and a few choice recipes, people will save it as a souvenir.

Music is a pleasant addition to the festivities. Even tapes will work. Strolling players or sit-down musicians in the gazebo add to the fun. You may want to investigate the possibility of a a speaker system too.

Good directions to the fair are paramount. A map on every flyer, plenty of signs along the road clearly marking every turn, and balloons or banners heralding the festival entrance are helpful.

Food can be catered or served by the local church ladies or a service club. It can be simple — herbed, of course — or a boxed herbal lunch by advance reservation only. If the day is hot, a lemonade stand will reap a bonanza. Encourage the vendor to use sprigs of lemon balm and sell herbal breads or cookies prepackaged in small baggies.

What about tables for your vendors? Should they bring their own or will you rent a supply of tables? Will you provide chairs? How about tents for sun or rain?

Additional amenities to consider are portable rest rooms, picnic tables, a child care concession, water stations, wagons to rent to serious buyers, and a herb information booth. I'm sure you can think of many others.

As with all such events, the success hinges on getting out the word. You risk failure without all the publicity possible. Send news releases to the media within a two-hundred-mile radius. Buy advertising if necessary, design a logo for posters, don't stint on flyers — distribute them everywhere and through every participant — send dates to national magazines that publish calendar of events listings, inform your state's tourism bureau. Whatever it takes to inform the public, do it. But don't keep your herb fair a secret, or it's a lot of work for a lot of people for naught.

It's Party Time: Open Your Doors

Just as inviting guests motivates you to clean and tidy your home, public celebrations encourage you to spiff up your herb shop. Schedule an open house and watch the activity begin! There's no better way to attract the public than to offer a free event.

First, the shop and garden need attention. You'll want the public to see a weed-free, well-labeled garden, a cheery, neatly arranged shop, cleared paths, special exhibits on the porch or in the garden shed, flowers throughout (potpourri in the bathroom), and fresh new curtains — nothing should escape your personal, careful attention. It's a party!

Add to this beautiful setting delicious foods, attractively presented with lots of herbs and edible flower garnishes. Toss in free recipes for the party treats you're serving, and everyone will go away with a souvenir bearing the name of your shop. One important bit of advice: *never* serve anything that doesn't contain something you sell. This is your golden opportunity to introduce people to your products — don't miss it!

People have endless questions about herbs, no doubt about it. Be prepared: have someone on hand to answer questions, such as yourself or a master gardener who specializes in herbs. Set up an information booth with a display of books, some well-labeled, potted plants, and pictures of herb gardens. At our events, we also set up a resource table in our garage workshop, which is specially swept and tidied for the occasion.

Because we want people to stay and truly enjoy our party, we also set up a VCR and chairs in the garage/workshop, so guests can rest a bit while nibbling on goodies and view one of the herbal tapes we have purchased.

Left on their own, viewers frequently rewind and reset the machine for us.

You should consider adding a special feature to your open house program, such as a local basket maker, wood-carver, radio personality, author with a book to sign, or a famous personage in the field of herbs (it may even be a member of your family). We usually work on this important addition to our open house a year in advance, so that the guest of honor can be adequately prepared for and catered to at the event. He or she is your ace — treat them well.

Expenses for an open house can mount up. Besides the obvious cost of food — the main focus of any party — there are the costs of hiring extra help, printing recipe favors (with our name and other announcements clearly evident), offering prizes, hosting an honored featured guest, and — most expensive — invitations and advertising. After all, what's a party without guests? Without the necessary publicity, we could be stuck with a lot of leftover food.

Publicize your event with flyers, bag stuffers, or invitations; offer them at every workshop, lecture, and meeting you attend. Make posters for public bulletin boards. Send announcements to every newspaper in your area. Your special feature, depending on what it is, may be the key to getting free publicity — always better than any paid advertising.

Offer door prizes and you will reap a harvest of names and addresses for your mailing list — well worth the price of the prizes. We usually select prize items such as books, that can be mailed to the lucky winner. The winning name can be selected at the end of the festivities, or do it every hour on the hour and people will linger waiting for the drawing.

We also give out individual gifts with our name on them, such as small nosegays, free seeds, or bookmarks.

On the day of your open house, use banners, bunting, and balloons to proclaim the event. Mount a special display on the sidewalk and fling the doors wide open. People driving by are sure to be drawn into the festivities.

An open house is a lot of work, but well worth it. We look at it as a party to entertain our old and faithful friends, while luring new customers into the fold. They will see us at our best, enjoy true herbal hospitality, and plan to come back as we show them clearly that "Herbs Make the Difference."

To Feed the Multitudes

Entertaining with food and drink is a natural extension of your herb business and a recipe for turning business into pleasure. In the beginning, we put the teapot on for a car full of visitors, an out-of-towner, or to cheer up a gloomy day. Herb teas were served casually, spur of the moment, while we tended the front desk. As business grew, we began offering herb tea parties for groups by appointment for a moderate fee. These were held in our workshop which was swept for the occasion and filled with lavish bouquets of fresh herbs. Lace covered our plywood workshop tables where we served herbal tidbits displayed on mirrors. With twinkling vigil light candles, we managed a degree of panache. The size of the budget has nothing to do with making a party memorable.

Now we have a tearoom where we serve customers with flair and elegance, sit-down style. A teapot cradled in a well-padded cozy is part of the service setting at each table. The price we charge depends upon the menu, ranging from simple to elaborate.

Our most challenging affairs are our Twice-a-TwelveMonth open house parties when we offer herbal refreshments to hundreds for free. In June, we serve on the porch, covering the large plywood potting table with a colorful sheet topped with lace or homespun and plying our guests with a large array of herbal treats.

Exciting, delicious recipes that can be made in large quantities on a budget are critical to the success of these occasions. Herbal businesses have a tremendous advantage when it comes to low-budget entertaining — herbs can rescue the most modest of dishes.

When we set our table, we set the stage for a party mood. We wrap silk scarves around jars, place wreaths of thyme around plates, tuck a teddy bear into the setting for fun, put out a

Herbal refreshments, labeled and set on a lavishly decorated table, set the mood for a successful open house.

few antiques to impress, or add a topiary or two for drama — touches that raise the lowly herbal fare to elegant proportions. M. F. K. Fisher, the food writer, recalls that the most impressive dish she was ever served was caviar surrounded with apple blossoms. We can do that.

Simple butters, herbal jellies, zesty mustards, tasty dips, bite-size cookies or sandwiches, and seasoned popcorn are foods we can manage for huge crowds on a tight budget. Herbal teas, served as punch over ice in June or hot in November, cost little more than the water used to steep them. We mix and match our herbal harvests to develop our own delicious blends, or brew a boxed tea off the store shelves that can be purveyed through sampling. Sometimes we serve spiced punch with cinnamon stick stirrers, iced in summer or kept hot in an electric cooking pot in winter.

No matter what the menu, we use as many herbs and spices as possible from The Rosemary House's inventory and we always, without exception, distribute free recipes so the party goers can duplicate all the good foods they have tasted using our products. Impressive pyramids and baskets of the blends are displayed throughout the shop, inviting purchases.

There are three cardinal rules for serving at these special public occasions:

1. Everything is to be presented gloriously with flair and a lavish use of herbs and edible flowers, on your best serving pieces.
2. Every dish must be herbal.
3. Every recipe requires a stand-up label such as a placecard.

We spend a lot of time planning our parties. The theme, color scheme, and menu are discussed for weeks before the event. We search for suitable recipes all year long, sample them and adjust them to our needs. When we have enough recipes, we print another cook-booklet to sell.

Chapter 8

EXPANDING YOUR BUSINESS AND MARKETS

BUYING WHOLESALE

EVENTUALLY YOUR BUSINESS MAY OUTGROW THE CAPACITY OF YOUR GARDEN, demanding more time and energy than you alone can provide. When you first start up, you have the time and desire to do it all. Fine! Great! Wonderful! That's the fun of it and you learn a lot. But there comes a time when you feel pulled in all directions at once. To maintain both shop and sanity, consider buying herbal product wholesale from others in the business. Almost everybody does it. Besides, it keeps us all busy.

Buying from other herbal producers provides a wider variety of items for your customers. For instance, we welcome hand-produced herbal soaps, dips, seasonings, and vinegars we don't make ourselves; clay products from the potter's kiln; and enticing herbal greeting cards designed by master calligraphers or gifted artists who love herbs as much as we do.

These delightful additions dress our shelves, complement our own Rosemary House products, lure our customers back again and again to see what's new, and leave us free to pursue other projects or products.

Our network of outside suppliers is kept busy supplying outlets across the country. If the product is unique, well-packaged, and the price is right, repeat orders will flow. We gladly buy from these talented people in quantity at wholesale.

Sometimes it's possible to work out a special deal where your name appears on the label. So much the better. We have several "private label" sources and are pleased to meet their high minimum-order requirement to be able to market another excellent item under our name.

We are all searching for clever new ideas in this business. It's rather amazing how many ways these ancient herbs can be used and reused. When you come upon a marketable way, be very careful not to infringe on someone's creativity verbatim. If there is already a wholesale source available, always strive to modify or perhaps improve the product before you market your own version in your shop.

In some rare instances, we even purchase products similar to those we produce ourselves — potpourris, dips, and teas for example — but different enough so that they complement rather than compete with ours. We enjoy being a part of the vast network of herbal producers, both buying and selling.

We also buy related mass-produced items that look good in the shop and always sell well: baskets; teapots and other accoutrements; gift and greeting cards; perfumes and herbal cosmetics; books, books, books; ceramic tiles or mugs; bee skeps, sundials, and other garden ornaments; windowsill gardens, seeds, and selected fertilizers; woks, quiche pans, and tin cookie cutters for the kitchen corner — the list is endless.

Seeking out what sells is part of the excitement. You may wish to attend a major gift show; many metropolitan areas have one or two a year — Dallas, Los Angeles, New York City, Chicago, Atlanta, Miami to name a few. A trade publication such as *Gifts and Decorative Accessories* (*see* "Resources") lists them all — even England, Spain, and Paris. (What a *great* tax deduction to go on a buying trip *abroad!*) They are an excellent source for dinnerware (called tabletop), basketry, collectibles, packaging supplies, as well as for inexhaustible ideas on future expansion.

The really large trade shows will admit only bona fide businesses, so go prepared with adequate ID such as your state resale tax number, business cards, and a list of credit references.

When you register to attend a show, you will receive a catalog/directory. It will pay for you to sit down in advance with a cup of coffee to peruse it and red-pencil the sources that interest you; it helps to go knowing what you want for your shop. If possible, plan a two-day stay — and wear comfortable shoes!

The first day, visit all the booths you marked, check out quality and prices, minimums (how many you must purchase to place a first order or open an account), and ask for literature. Watch for "Show Specials" which can be a really good deal, with a larger profit margin, but only if it's something you can merchandise successfully. Mark down the numbers of the booths you are interested in, lest you never find them again. Then, on the second day, after you have reviewed the bewildering amount of information and sorted it all out in your head, go back to place your orders. Be selective.

Getting many shipments at once can be chaotic, so it's good to stagger the shipping dates, spacing each order a week or two apart. First orders with a company are usually shipped COD — that's cash on delivery, so arrange your finances accordingly. Credit takes more time and can be established later.

Gift show inventory can be a major expense, easily getting out of hand. We like to save up our Christmas profits to reinvest at one of the winter gift shows. It is an exciting way to restock a few new things while we busily work to replace all our old standbys. Consider your purchases carefully and don't ever overextend yourself financially. Most of all, as you make your selection, never — never! — lose sight of your herb garden. These are the products that make your shop stand out, the backbone of your business, the fragrant magical herbs that lured you into all this in the first place.

SELLING WHOLESALE

If you are creating herbal products — mixing herbal seasonings, and packaging and labeling your own products — and you are looking for a larger market, then *you* can become the wholesaler. We have discovered this to be a good way to go and have learned a few things along the torturous way. If you choose to take this route to profits, perhaps my suggestions will smooth your pathway to success.

Once we hit on a winning seasoning mix, we prepare it in quantity in a new, twenty-five-pound lard can. Since we don't want it to go stale before it's all sold, we sell it in single packages to walk-in customers, but we also market it by the dozens of packages to our wholesale customers. This really keeps the product moving.

To make a wholesale venture profitable, pricing is paramount. We figure our price based on the total costs of our new product, including the herbs used, whether from the garden or purchased, the cost of packaging and the label, the estimated time and labor involved, plus a bit more — at least 10 percent — for overhead.

Our labor costs include the pay for outside workers. Almost all of our packaging is farmed out to people willing to do piecework in their homes on their own timetable. Their pay depends on the complexity of the packaging: ten cents each for a simple baggie and bow; twenty-five cents each for a kit containing several parts. We ask our homeworkers to time themselves in order to arrive at a mutually agreed upon hourly rate, based on the number of pieces done per hour. Pay checks are sent out upon their completion and return of a staggering number of packages.

Using the actual cost of our new item as a base, we shelf test the product to complete our pricing decision. Does the package catch our customers' eyes? Does it move out quickly? We have had bright ideas that languished on the shelves, eventually to disappear and never be seen again. The price is usually about three times the actual cost of the item, but sometimes a really nifty item that flies off the shelves is priced at a four-time markup.

For example, let's deal in round figures and suppose our new Tra-la-la Salad Seasoning costs us $1 a package to manufacture, everything included. We market it at $3, or perhaps $4 if the packaging is particularly eye-catching. That allows us to sell individual pieces slowly at a good profit and to wholesale it quickly by the dozen (no less) for $1.50 or $2 each, again at a fair profit, depending upon the volume sold.

Once you develop your wholesale terms, stick with them. You can always devise special deals for assorted dozens, three or more of a variety, or a greater quantity discount. You may want to offer free postage on orders over $100. We can reduce prices for first-time orders on some of our items, such as self-published books, but we can't on most things.

In turn, our wholesale customers can sell our products at the same prices we do, $3 or $4 each. However, that's their decision; we have seen our products sold at much higher markups.

Because we have developed a complete line of Rosemary House products over the years, we now list them in a wholesale catalog, which you may request. We also take our line to trade shows such as the International Herb Growers and Marketers Association convention, where we show and sell along with many other related suppliers.

We have shown our product line to wholesalers at a few major gift shows as well, in Washington, New York, and Atlanta. There are gift shows in every area of the country, and you may want to attend a few (*see* pages 154 – 55. If you go to sell, know that booth rent is very expensive and the days are strenuous to boot. But through exposure at these shows we have sold our herbs to many gift shops, and museum and restoration shops, and expanded our wholesale territory far beyond Mechanicsburg and Pennsylvania.

Another way to wholesale is through independent sales representatives. We have also employed "a rep" to take our products on the road. These representatives are freelance salespeople who go from shop to shop showing and selling many different lines of goods. They depend upon large quantity sales to make a living plus their expenses. They charge an additional 15 percent for their services, which we figure into our pricing too. Once a rep has opened a market, they charge the 15 percent fee for all repeat orders you receive from that customer in the mail or over the phone.

Even when we are on vacation, we are representing The Rosemary House. A traveling wholesale sample basket sits ready in our car at all times. In different areas of the country, we seek out possible outlets for our line. We just check the local Yellow Pages under "Herbs," then pay the businesses listed there a visit. It's a fun way to see other herbal enterprises, and sometimes we even get an order. In any case, making the call gives us a legitimate business expense tax deduction.

How busy do you want to be? Wholesaling is worth consideration if you are willing to invest the time and money up front. It has certainly been profitable for us. Wholesale orders account for a good one-third of our business. The UPS delivery person comes to our shop everyday, taking out a pile of orders going to other shops, as well as bringing in a few for us from other wholesalers.

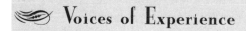 Voices of Experience

MURPHY CREEK FARM
CONNIE LAWRANCE

"Being at home, I have more time for my family while working at a job I really enjoy and making a decent profit," says Connie Lawrance. Thirty acres and an 1875 schoolhouse on the banks of Murphy Creek in Madrid, Iowa make up

Connie's home-based wholesale wreath and craft business. Begun years ago in her kitchen, with a spare bedroom and garage for storage, Connie now has a workshop, a greenhouse, and a flower drying shed.

She first sold potpourri from her backyard gardens to friends and at craft shows. Through an Iowa state–sponsored home-based business seminar, Connie met a sales representative who introduced her to the wholesale business.

She marketed her potpourri in tiny two-inch rag baskets she learned to make in a craft class. Thus The Rag Merchant was born and took off into serious wholesaling with seven salespersons and seven pieceworkers helping her. Despite success, Connie's tired hands told her there wasn't enough profit in this project. So she went back to the garden and drying flowers to sell in bunches to shops. But to her surprise, she discovered that stores preferred her wreaths and other designs to loose flowers.

Having moved to the bounty of Murphy Creek Farm where she tends a quarter of an acre of herbs and flowers, Connie now supplies several stores — a mall shop, a massage therapy tearoom/gift shop in downtown Des Moines, and several smaller accounts. She makes frames from wild vines, grows and gathers all the wreath materials, and designs each piece. At Christmastime she sells forty to fifty wreaths a week.

CATS IN THE CRADLE
CHRIS WITTMANN

Soap maker, herb gardener, musician, author, and lecturer, Chris Wittmann operates her wholesale soap and herbal botanicals business out of her home in rural New Hampshire, which she shares with twenty-three cats. She augments her income by writing articles for herbal publications, and plans to start work on a book. "That is," she adds, "if I can teach my cats to make soap!"

Always intrigued by the healing properties of plants, Chris drew on her twenty-five years of research and the knowledge passed down through family traditions to develop rich herbal soaps, hand creams, emollient healing salves, and other products made from organically grown botanicals. Attractively wrapped and well labeled, her soaps proclaim to be "kind to the Earth and to your skin." Her soap-making operation is based in a nineteenth-century farmhouse and uses her garden herbs along with the by-products of hives: honey, beeswax, and propolis. At Christmastime, Chris adds golden beeswax ornaments made in antique molds to her line.

Her gardener's hand soap is a necessity for every daughter of the earth with work-weary hands. Pure, natural, and superfatted, her soaps and salves are laden with soothing healing herbs, including aloe vera, comfrey, calendula, rosehip seed oil, elder, yellow dock, violet leaves, St. John's wort, lavender, myrrh, benzoin, goldenseal, plantain, sage, and marshmallow.

Chris also offers workshops on the use and properties of medicinal herbs, gives garden tours, lectures on historically accurate plantings, and consults on planning a herbal tea garden.

She has a distributor who markets only products made in New Hampshire, and several national mail-order catalog businesses have shown interest in carrying her products.

HERB'S HERBS
SANDIE SHORES

Blessed with youth and stamina, Sandie Shores runs a very successful business in fresh-cut herbs, edible flowers, and potted plants — all at wholesale. There is no retail shop to divert her from her main interests: growing and marketing.

Located near the well-populated city of Rochester, Minnesota, Sandie serves eighteen restaurant accounts, ranging in value from $50 to $1,200 monthly. After several years of building this base, Sandie can now count on $2,500 monthly from these accounts. In the spring, she wholesales forty-five varieties of herb plants to area nurseries, selling a total of ten thousand plants.

Of her success, Sandie says, "It took untold hours of research and hard work up front. My main challenge was learning to grow, package, and market fresh-cut herbs commercially."

After five years in business, Sandie expanded her operation to include selling fresh herbs to four local supermarkets, the largest one of which buys $400 worth of herbs a week. Instead of using hard plastic trays, Sandie developed a relatively "green" environmentally safe package for these sales.

She discovered yet another market recently — the farmers' market, where she was amazed at the money her fresh herbs generated.

Sandie's garden has grown with her business. After two years of operation, Herb's Herbs purchased the farm across the road and moved their thirty- by seventy-six-foot greenhouse.

Plans are underway to build another large greenhouse for winter growing of annuals that are now grown outdoors and harvested only in summer. With this advance, Sandie will be able to supply all her accounts year-round.

Herb Gathering, Inc.
Paula A. Winchester

Paula Winchester's business began with a request for fresh herbs from a four-star restaurant. She started enlisting the help of herb growers, and before long was building an herb empire, including growing, merchandising, warehousing, packaging, and delivery operations. Paula pulled together about thirty growers, one commercial, but all eager. "In the beginning we were all in this stewpot together. There were few commercial operations around like this one from which to learn," says Paula. Today Herb Gathering, Inc. sells fresh herbs to restaurants and supermarkets throughout the Kansas City/St. Louis, Missouri area.

They produce eighteen fresh herbs in winter and up to thirty-five in the summer, for the up-scale market of gourmet foods as well as crafts and bouquets.

Among other endeavors, for over a decade the consortium of growers has held a herb plant sale which occupies eight thousand square feet and sells twenty thousand plants in five hours.

At the same time, Paula has been building her own business. After enthusiastically expanding in all directions for several years, she downsized into a leaner operation. She sold off a mail-order seed catalog she had developed, which specialized in French vegetables and edible flowers. She also operated a herbal gift shop for several years, an experience that taught her she really enjoyed mail-order sales and craft shows best of all. Today, she limits her own business to herbal crafts, sold both wholesale and retail along with the fresh herbs.

CATALOG SALES

If no one but the mail carrier walks through the door at The Rosemary House, we are still very much in business. We can count on receiving at least one mail order every day. Because our shop is off the beaten path, mail order has become vitally important to our business.

You might say that we fell into catalog sales at the request of our customers. Many years ago, when we were quite new to the ways of the world of business, we promoted our products through craft shows. The biggest show we did was at Hershey Dutch Days, in Hershey, Pennsylvania; tourists flocked from everywhere to this celebration. Many of them admired our new herb stand, and asked repeatedly, "Can we mail order your things?"

It didn't take us long to realize we had a market right there waiting for us — all we needed was a catalog. That very night I sat typing into the wee hours, listing every product I could think of, and adding an enticing sentence or two to describe it. There was no time for artwork; I just used words to lure sales.

Early the next morning, I raced the copy to our local chamber of commerce where they did mimeographing. We took a hundred copies of our new catalog to Hershey for the second day of the show; we sold them for a mere twenty-five cents each, the cost of production. In the meantime, the chamber of commerce was cranking out more copies for us to sell the rest of the week. Thus, our catalog sales department was born.

People in The Rosemary House's hometown of Mechanicsburg, Pennsylvania, wonder what keeps us alive while major stores on Main Street are going out of business one by one. The answer, of course, is herbs; they make the difference. But mail order has really been our salvation. Before the rest of the world finally got the word and beat a path to our door, the mailman was forging the way bringing in mail orders that kept us going.

Over the years our little mimeographed catalog has changed, but not dramatically. It is now thirty-six pages printed and collated by the thousands on a high-speed press, and we have added cunning little sketches to our word descriptions — but its folksy, homemade flavor remains. We have considered upgrading it, but economics and common sense keep us on the same track. We have never mailed our catalog out willy-nilly. To make the mailing economical, every request must meet the break-even fee (i.e., bring in a minimum amount of sales), so we cannot afford to send it out indiscriminately like another piece of junk mail. We have built a list of mail-order customers who save their catalogs and use them over and over. Some even purchase our catalogs as gifts for their friends!

Convenient, mail-order buying is gaining in customer popularity. Consider Lillian Vernon, the leader in the field, who has ten million catalog customers. Begun in 1951 with a $2,000 investment, Ms. Vernon's business has enjoyed phenomenal success. She started with a small ad in a national magazine and four years later produced her first catalog. Customer loyalty has been built with a guaranteed send-it-back, no-questions-asked policy.

If you start a mail-order catalog, you need to develop a good system for filling the orders. Our staff is kept busy getting orders off to the customers quickly and correctly. We keep our mailing costs down by recycling sturdy cartons, packing peanuts, and wrapping paper. Whatever comes in with a shipment is promptly recycled in the mail-order department. It has become a point of pride with us that our only shipping overhead cost is mailing tape. The customer, as is usual, pays postage costs.

Happenstance may have pulled us into catalog sales, but satisfied customers have kept us there. Over the years we have been fortunate enough to be listed as a reputable source for herb plants and products in national magazines and several books. Such solid-gold advertising, frequently unsolicited, keeps us going and growing. If sales are slow, try mail order but be assured that it is not going to be an overnight success. With aggressive marketing and patience, however, it can become a major part of any herb business.

THE MAGICK GARDEN
LINDA GANNON, THE FAERIE QUEEN

When all the products she had made from her herb garden were sold at an open house party, Linda Gannon decided then and there that she could "turn all this fun into profit."

The mother of two young children, Linda was on leave from her teaching job; tending her herb garden provided the perfect diversion. She loved every aspect of it — planting, weeding, harvesting and, most of all, making small treasures. Creating herb wreaths, herb and flower arrangements, tussie mussies, and potpourris kept her busy.

With the renovation of an old building on her farm in Wisconsin, The Little Farm Workshoppe was born. For seven years Linda made and sold her herbal creations while reading all she could find on herbs, taking classes and workshops, and experimenting with different preservation techniques.

Linda's readings mysteriously guided her to magical herbalism, drawing her in like an invisible force. Soon she was deeply immersed in whimsical creations, amulets, magical brews, ointments, salves, incense, glitz, and glitter. The Magick Garden thus was born, and Linda began creating Magical Gift Baskets, calling herself "The Faerie Queen."

> *My favorite times in the garden were full-moon summer nights, when the crickets chanted and the warm, soft air was perfumed with the rich sweet honeysuckle. Everything was glowing silver, reflecting the moonlight . . . there was a luxuriousness in moon basking on the rich green carpet, watching the clouds glide across the moon . . . I felt like a faerie princess in her royal garden!*
>
> Linda Gannon of
> The Magick Garden

The focus of her business evolved further to aromatherapy and perfumery. Now Linda is marketing the most exquisite potpourris you can imagine. Touched with "faerie magick" (she prefers the archaic spelling), moondust and glitter, they cast spells. She has given up her shop and dropped her demanding newsletter to focus on blending and selling her beribboned, boxed potpourri presentations through The Magick Garden mail-order catalog.

PINE CREEK HERBS
KATHLEEN GIPS

Author of a comprehensive floral dictionary, Kathleen Gips has developed a life work that has the depth and beauty of one huge, eloquent tussie mussie. Captured by *The Language of Flora,* she specializes in making fragrant tussie mussies to order, and selling related books, hard-to-find posy holders, all sorts of Victorian herbal accessories, and handcrafted herbal products. When zoning regulations prevented her from opening a shop in her home in Chagrin Falls, Ohio, Kathleen launched her unique catalog — *The Nostalgic Nosegay.* She has an extensive inventory, producing almost everything from her own garden's harvest. Over five hundred jars of delicious herbal jellies, another five hundred bottles of exciting flavored vinegars, countless pounds of aromatic potpourris, and a seemingly never-ending supply of pretty nosegays tailored to all occasions are turned out every year.

With no store to mind, Kathleen is free to work her gardens, speak to many organizations, teach classes, serve the local herb society, and continue her endless research into the ancient secrets of flowers while she tends to her family.

Her small-town garden is a tapestry of colors and scents exuding hidden meanings. The front yard is surrounded by a hundred rose bushes; the terraced backyard boasts culinary, tussie mussie, and potpourri gardens. A "no-care" shade garden for relaxing; a secret garden hidden in the rugosa roses; a formal rose bed with rose hedge and arbor; a knot garden; a Peter Rabbit garden with miniature vegetables; a thyme garden around a mill stone; and container gardening on the deck where she has more sun for basils and annual flowers round out Kathleen's collection. As she readily admits, there is little room for grass!

HOME PARTIES

Everyone loves a party and a herbal party is magical. It coaxes friends into the ancient circle of lore and legends of the fascinating useful herb.

In-house merchandise parties have become popular; however, in this case once again "Herbs Make the Difference." At an herbal home party you offer a private lecture and demonstration of your products; your fee is paid through the guests' purchases.

Whether you have a shop or only do craft fairs, you can post an inviting sign that will catch the eye of potential hostesses for such a pleasurable event. The hostess invites a minimum of ten friends, neighbors, and family members — and more if her home will accommodate them and you can handle the group comfortably — who will provide a personalized group, large enough to generate interest, questions, and sales.

You may wish to offer your hostess a special gift or gift certificate for her efforts, with the value based on a percentage of the sales made in the course of the party.

Unless the hostess prefers to invite guests over the phone, you might also provide her with inexpensive printed herbal invitations to mail. These can be the size of regular postcards, and offer you an initial opportunity to introduce your business and herbal products in an enticing manner. Allow room for your hostess's name, address, and the time of the party, and the rest of the space is yours. Be clever! Offer to give out free recipes, prizes, tips, hints, and to answer questions about the wonders of the world of herbs.

You can have invitations and recipe sheets printed in quantity at low cost, and write it off as a necessary business expense, another form of advertising. Just be sure your shop logo, address, hours of operation, and the copyright-free "Herbs Make the Difference" logo (*see* Appendix) are on there somewhere.

Encourage your hostess to serve herbal treats by offering her well-tested, inexpensive recipes for herb tea (of course), hot or iced, tasty dips, finger sandwiches, and spicy cookies. If some of the foods served contain dip mixes or seasonings you are purveying, so much the better. Why not provide the garnishes and centerpiece from your herb garden? These lovely additions will generate the conversation you need to build your business enterprise.

During the party, show your herbal wares — vinegars, jellies, bath products, potpourris, sachets, pressed flower notepapers, wreaths, and other crafts. Give every guest an order sheet and paper in advance (ask for a name and address on each order for your mailing list file), so they can record their selections. You may bring items to be purchased on the spot or arrange to deliver and distribute orders through the hostess — it's your choice.

Remind guests of the special gift potential in these unique herbal offerings, and be sure to exhibit a pretty basketful topped with a bunch of dried herbs and a bow. Emphasize that baskets can be tailored to personal occasions and holidays throughout the year. One great way to market your made-to-order herbal gift basket service is to develop a special flyer on baskets to distribute at parties offering convenient phone shopping for everyone.

Weave a little lore around each item you speak about. By speaking enthusiastically and educating your audience, you will encourage more sales. People are entranced by legends, fragrance, symbolism, ancient magical usage, and all the hidden virtues that set herbs apart from everything else on earth. Where does the herb come from? What does it do? Indispensable to the castle of old, how does it fit into my twentieth-century lifestyle? Make your listeners want it! Sales will follow.

Once you do a party or two, you will learn in no time what sells and what doesn't, as well as how to price the merchandise for your area. Well-made crafts are always in demand and command a premium. Catnip toys never go out of style. Foods, especially if you provide tiny samples, are appealing and guarantee repeat sales. Eventually, you may wish to add essential oils and other supplies for crafters and do-it-yourselfers.

Offer prizes, which can be as simple as surplus from your garden — a potted plant, a bunch of yarrow, a quart of dried mint, or a colorful, fragrant tussie mussie in season. Again tell about the wonder of each, tuck in a recipe or a photocopied article about your prize. *Remember:* no one was born knowing all this, and if the prizewinner doesn't know what to do with the prize, it has little value. I'll bet you will take orders for some of your goodwill prizes, especially those charming nosegays. Who can resist them?

Before you leave any party, and preferably before refreshments are served, sign up one of the attendees to host the next party. If you have a lively informative session with an exciting display of wares not readily available elsewhere, delicious easy herbal refreshments, and the entice-ment of a reward for the hostess, you can perpetuate your business through the home party plan.

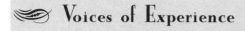

Voices of Experience

MERRY MEADOW FARM
GRAYCE J. MOOREHEAD

Having started her business with $50 in 1984, Grayce Moorehead measures her success by the number of customers who say they want a shop just like hers, which is sometimes as many as three a day.

Her lifelong fascination with herbs and everlastings, nur-tured by living on her grandfather's wholesale/retail flower farm, and having a mother who was a top floral designer, helped prepare Grayce for her business creating dried flower pieces. She combined her backgrounds in interior design and mathematics with a love of gardening and artistic abilities to create Merry Meadow Farm in Wickford, Rhode Island.

Grayce began her business with wreath parties in other people's homes. Special orders, and even mail orders, soon followed. A $5,000 special order propelled her out of her cluttered home and into a tiny shop, which she soon outgrew. "The business became a roller coaster ride going in all direc-tions," says Grayce.

She wrote down everything she could do, wouldn't do, and all the issues to consider in selecting a location for a bigger store, and finally decided to make her move in 1990, just as the New England economy took a deep plunge. "People were in the worst mood I hope I ever have to cope with," says Grayce.

Her business is prospering in an old Victorian with six showrooms, a workroom and storage space, in the tourist area of Wickford, Rhode Island. Her gross income has tripled since the move! Although she juggles everything that needs to be done to maintain a shop seven days a week, success is hers. "Not easy," Grayce admits. "People who work forty hours a week don't know what they are missing."

RESOURCES

These organizations and periodicals are all excellent resources for herb lovers and businesses.

ORGANIZATIONS

The American Botanical Council
P.O. Box 201660
Austin, TX 78720

American Herb Association
P.O. Box 1673
Nevada City, CA 95959
(Membership includes *AHA Quarterly.*)

The Herb Research Foundation
1007 Pearl St., Suite 200
Boulder, CO 80302

The Herb Society of America, Inc.
9019 Kirtland Chardon Road
Mentor, OH 44060

The International Herb Growers
and Marketers Association
1202 Allanson Road
Mundelein, IL 60060

SCORE (Service Corps of Retired Executives)
Check the telephone directory for the local chapter of this free, tax-supported volunteer organization. Or write to:
U.S. Small Business Administration
409 3rd St., S.W.
Washington, D.C. 20416

Small Business Service Bureau, Inc.
National Operations Center
554 Main St.
P.O. Box 1441
Worcester, MA 01601

PERIODICALS

Business of Herbs *
R.R. 2, Box 246
Shevlin, MN 56676

The Flora-Line
Berry Hill Press
7336 Berry Hill
Palos Verdes, CA 90274

Foster's Botanical and Herb Review
Steven Foster
P.O. Box 106
Eureka Springs, AR 72632

Gift and Decorative Accessories *
51 Madison Avenue
New York, NY 10160
(Lists all major national and
international gift shows.)

The Herb Companion
Interweave Press
201 E. Fourth St.
Loveland, CO 80537

The Herb Quarterly
P.O. Box 689
San Anselmo, CA 94960

*The Herb, Spice, and Medicinal
Plant Digest*
Department of Plant and Soil Sciences
University of Massachusetts
Amherst, MA 01003

The Herbal Connection * (The Herb
Growing and Marketing Network)
P.O. Box 245
Silver Spring, PA 17575

The Herbal Gazette
Betty Wold and Barbara Downs
Rt. 1, Box 576
Checotah, OK 74426

Herban Lifestyles
Christine Utterback
84 Carpenter Rd.
New Hartford, CT 06057

Potpourri from Herbal Acres
Pine Row Publications
Box 428
Washington Crossing, PA 18977

*Wholesale Sources

SOURCES

Close-at-hand sources for many of your needs can be found by checking the Yellow Pages of the telephone book of your nearest large city. You will find wholesale florists for ribbons and floral craft materials; paper and packaging suppliers who carry bags, boxes, tissue paper, and the like; printers for your business cards, stationery, product labels, booklets, flyers; and wholesale grocers with bulk herbs, spices, and extracts. Check out prices, minimum quantities you must buy, quality, and hours of operation. Be prepared to use your retail license number, a bank reference, and any other proof you have of being a legitimate business in order to gain access to wholesale sources. We also depend on others who offer mail-order services. You will find many additional wholesale sources among the organizations and periodicals listed under Resources especially the Business of Herbs and The Herbal Connection..

BASKETS

Basketville
Main Street
Box 710
Putney, VT 05346
802-387-5509

Creative Art Flowers, Inc.
Box 11367
85 Commerce Dr.
Hauppauge, NY 11788
800-645-9446
516-435-2727

Nowco International, Inc.
1 George Ave.
Wilkes-Barre, PA 18705
800-233-8302
717-822-5255

Peterboro Basket Co.
130 Grove Street
Peterborough, NH 03458
603-924-3861

Royal Cathay
2019 E. Monk Vista Ave.
Vacaville, CA 95688
800-388-8890

United Basket Co., Inc.
58-01 Grand Ave.
Maspeth, NY 11378
718-894-5454

Willow Specialties
68 Nassau St.
Rochester, NY 14605
800-724-7300

BOOKS (FOR RESALE)

Crown Publishers/Outlet Book Co., Inc.
201 E. 50th St.
New York City, NY 10022
212-751-2600

Dover Publications, Inc.
31 E. 2nd St.
Mineola, NY 11501
516-294-7000

New Leaf Distributing Co.
5425 Tulane Dr., S.W.
Atlanta, GA 30336
404-691-6996

Rodale Press
33 E. Minor St.
Emmaus, PA 18098
215-967-5171

Storey Communications, Inc.
Schoolhouse Road
Pownal, VT 05261
800-827-8673

BOTTLES, JARS, AND SUCH

Boone Drug Co.
617 West King St.
Boone, NC 28607
704-264-3766

Lavender Lane
6715 Donerail Dr.
Sacramento, CA 95842
916-334-4400

DRIED HERBS AND FLOWERS

Cramers' Posie Patch
116 Trail Rd. North
Elizabethtown, PA 17022
717-367-9494

Homestead Gardens
Pumpkin Hill Rd.
Warner, NH 03278
603-456-2258

Sunburst Bottle
7001 Sunburst Way
Citrus Heights, CA 95621
916-722-4632

Spencer Farms
4675 Bender Rd.
Middleville, MI 49333
616-795-7815

Woodfield Whimsies
P.O. Box 184
Ashippun, WI 53003
414-474-4149

GENERAL MERCHANDISE

New York Gift Fair
George Little Management, Inc.
10 Bank St., Suite 1200
White Plains, NY 10606
800-272-SHOW

HERB PLANTS
wholesale, through the mail

Bluebird Nursery, Inc.
P.O. Box 460
Clarkson, NE 68629
800-356-9164

Companion Plants
7247 N. Coolville Ridge Rd.
Athens, OH 45701
614-592-4643

Taylor's Gardens, Inc.
1535 Lone Oak Rd.
Vista, CA 92084
619-727-3485

HERBS, SPICES, BOTANICALS, AND OILS

Aphrodisia
62 Kent St.
Brooklyn, NY 11222
718-383-3677

Frontier Cooperative Herbs
Box 299
Norway, IA 52318
800-669-3275

Lorann Oils
4518 Aurelius Rd.
P.O. Box 22009
Lansing, MI 48909
517-882-0215

San Francisco Herb & Natural Food
1010 46th St.
Emeryville, CA 94608
510-547-6345

PACKAGING, BAGS, BOXES, AND SUPPLIES

Associated Bag Co.
400 W. Boden St.
Milwaukee, WI 53207
414-769-1000

Chiswick
33 Union Ave.
Sudbury, MA 01776
800-225-8708

Disbrow Envelope Corp. (seed envelope specialists)
25 Linden Ave., East
Jersey City, NJ 07305
201-434-2100

National Bag Co., Inc.
2233 Old Mill Rd.
Hudson, OH 44236
216-425-2600

NEBS
500 Main St.
Groton, MA 01471
800-225-6380

Spring-Fill Industries
P.O. Box 280
Hinesburg, VT 05461
800-688-8863

RIBBONS

Brooklyn Bow and Ribbon Co.
150 Denton Ave.
P.O. Box 508
Lynbrook, NY 11563
516-887-4600

Lion Ribbon Co.
100 Metro Way
Secaucus, NJ 07096
201-348-4500

R.B. Howell Co.
630 N.W. 10th Ave.
Portland, OR 97209
800-547-0368

UNIFORMS, APRONS

logo imprints

S. & H. Uniform Corp.
200 William St.
Port Chester, NY 10573
914-937-6800

HERB BUSINESSES

Here are the addresses for the herb businesses whose stories are told throughout this book. When you're in their neighborhoods, make sure you pay them a visit. Call first to be sure they are open.

Alloway Gardens And Herb Farm
Barbara Steele and Marlene Lufriu
456 Mud College Road
Littlestown, PA 17340
717-359-4548
717-359-4363

Arie's Herb Gardens
Penny Moore and Wanda Rayfield
300 Pineview Road
Sylacauga, AL 35150
205-249-8199

Back of The Beyond
Shash Georgi
7233 Lower East Hill Road
Colden, NY 14033
716-652-0427

Berry Hill Press
Dody Lyness
7336-S Berry Hill
Palos Verdes, CA 90274
213-377-7040

Bertoldi's Cedar Hill Gardens
David and Deborah Bertoldi
R.D. #1, Box 326
Freemansville Road
Reading, PA 19607
215-777-0178

Brier Rose Herbs
Mark and Rose Buras
202 Avenue A
Belle Chase, LA 70037
504-391-0019

Buffalo Springs Herb Farm
Don Haynie and Thom Hamlin
Rte 1, Box 476
Raphine, VA 24472
703-348-1083

Cats in the Cradle
Chris Wittmann
Rte 140
Alton, NH 03809
603-875-7284

Cellar Babies by Johanna's
JoAnne Fajack
2575 Dogwood Drive
Youngstown, OH 44511
216-793-9523

Country Petals Herbal Pottery
Sharon Magee
2724 Carsins Run Road
Aberdeen, MD 21001
410-836-2100

Countryside Samplings
Alice M. Prall
19 Countryside Drive
Brodsheadsville, PA 18322
717-992-2170

England's Herb Farm
Yvonne England
R.D. #1, Box 706
Todd and White School House Roads
Honey Brook, PA 19344
610-273-2863

Green Horizon Farm Herb Shop
Constance Miller
100 Guy's Lane
Bloomsburg, PA 17815
717-389-1040

Greenfield Herb Garden
ArLene and Pat Shannon
Depot and Harrison Streets
P.O. Box 439
Shipshewana, IN 46565
219-768-7110

Healing Heart Herbals
Cindy Parker
Box 8651
Newark, OH 43058
614-323-3278

Heart's Ease
Sharon Lovejoy
4101 Burton Drive
Cambria, CA 93428
800-266-HERB (4372)

The Herb Barn
Nancy J. Johns
1955 Greenley Avenue
Benton Harbor, MI 49022
616-927-2044

Herb Gathering, Inc.
Paula A. Winchester
5742 Kenwood Avenue
Kansas City, MO 64110
816-523-2653

The Herb Merchant
Timothy L. Newcomer and
Paul T. Mertel
70 W. Pomfret Street
Carlisle, PA 17013
717-249-0970

Herb's Herbs
Sandie Shores
Rt. 1, Box 128A
Zumbro Falls, MN 55991
507-753-2177

Hill Country Wreaths
Susan Wittig Albert
P.O. Drawer M
Bertram, TX 78605

Hi-On-A-Hill Herb Farm
Ruth S. Pacheco
836 Old Smithfield Road
North Smithfield, RI 02896
401-766-1408

Honey Rock Herb Farm
Dee and Jim Brown
P.O. Box 23
113 Honey Rock Way
Louisville, TN 37777
615-984-0954

Honeysuckle Lane
Linda Cook and Barbara Goodman
8275 Lithopolis Road
Carroll, OH 43112
614-837-5252

Ladybug Press
Lane Furneaux
7348 Lane Park Court
Dallas, TX 75225
214-368-4235

The Lavender House
Caroline Moss
445 Lode Lane
Solihull
West Midlands
B 928NS England
021-743-9205

Long Creek Herbs
Jim Long
Rt. 4, Box 730
Oak Grove, AR 72660
417-779-5450

The Magick Garden
Linda Gannon, the Faerie Queen
5703 Country Walk
McFarland, WI 53558

Mari-Mann Herb Co., Inc.
Maribeth Johnson
N. End of St. Louis Bridge Road
RR #4, Box 7
Decatur, IL 62521
217-429-1555

Maryland's Herb Basket
Maryland Miles Massey
399 Hazel Lane, Box 131
Millington, MD 21651
410-928-3301

Meadow Everlastings
Sharon Challand
16464 Shabbona Road
Malta, IL 60150
815-825-2539

Merry Meadow Farm
Grayce J. Moorehead
10 Phillips St. (Scenic 1A)
Wickford, RI 02852
401-294-3939

Murphy Creek Farm
Connie Lawrance
1257 Zookspur Road
Madrid, IA 50156
515-795-2215

Penny's Garden
Penny and Don Melton
P.O. Box 305
Black Creek Road
Mountain City, GA 30562
706-746-6918

Pine Creek Herbs
Kathleen Gips
152 S. Main Street
Chagrin Falls, OH 44022
216-247-5014

Quality Of Life Associates
Carol Corio
4 Field Road
Arlington, MA 02174
617-648-8343

The Rosemary House
120 S. Market Street
Mechanicsburg, PA 17055
717-697-5111

Shady Side Herbs
Amy Hinman-Shade
P.O. Box 190459
Hungry Horse, MT 59919
406-387-4184

Shale Hill Farm And Herb Gardens
Patricia K. Reppert
134 Hommelville Road
Saugerties, NY 12477
914-246-6982

Sinking Springs Herb Farm
Ann and Bill Stubbs
234 Blair Shore Road
Elkton, MD 21921
410-398-5566

Spoutwood Farm
Rob and Lucy Wood
R.D. #3, Box 66
Glen Rock, PA 17327
717-235-6610

The Squire's Herbary
Judith Merritt
1928 Walnut Street
Allentown, PA 18104
215-937-3610

Sunshine Herbs
Denise and Bryon Provencher
359 Kenoza Street
Haverhill, MA 01830
508-372-9798

A Thyme To Plant Herb Farm, Inc.
Bill and Marianne Ritchie
2523 Huguenot Springs Road
Midlothian, VA 23113
804-379-0653

Walton's Herbal Wares
Linda Walton
1280 Wilmer Road
Wentzville, MO 63385
314-327-8976

What Cheer Herbs
Janet and John Balletto
151 Tidewater Drive
Warwick, RI 02889
401-732-1009

Whiskey Run Herb Farm
Mary Schenck
188 Locktown-Flemington Road
Flemington, NJ 08822
908-782-1278

Wild Rose Herbs
Sue and John Thaxter
HCR 2, Box 1040
Hollister, MO 65672
417-335-2792

COPYRIGHT-FREE ARTWORK

This slogan and logo was the winning entry in a nationwide contest initiated by *Business of Herbs* magazine. All herb businesses are encouraged to use it freely to promote their own products and the herb industry in general. We use it on everything, especially all our seed packets. It's here for you to reproduce and use on T-shirts, bags, displays, and bumper stickers.

Suggested Reading

MY FAVORITE HERBALS — A FIVE-INCH BOOKSHELF

A herbal, modern or otherwise, is not always easy reading. Delightful, yes. Cover to cover nonstop reading, no. There is so much to absorb at one sitting. Perhaps this accounts for the present popularity of glossy picture books. The breathtaking photography, another form of "instant gratification," captures and dazzles the imagination while the pages fly by, creating a spectacular read.

Although I enjoy the newer publications — who doesn't? — it is my oldies but good, good, goodies that I turn to again and again. They nourish my hobby as none other, inform me, delight me, sometimes astonish me. Each one has a different flavor.

Decades ago I bought *The Home Garden Book of Herbs and Spices* by Milo Miloradovich (circa 1952), my first herbal. I knew I would never learn all it held, so much information and no pictures for relief. A slim, small volume of 236 pages covering Alecost to Zedoary — 34 pages of index! — I despaired at this overwhelming font of herbal knowledge. Little bit by little bit I nibbled away at it and eventually found it making an impact. Now I'm glad to say Milo's book, as crammed with with good solid information as ever, is available as an inexpensive Dover reprint.

In 1964, I acquired Adelma Simmons brand-new *Herb Gardening in Five Seasons,* another herbal delight of rich variety and practical influence. Slightly fatter with larger print, wonderful sketches of the herbs, and a few pictures to study, it was exciting to discover that the "fifth season" is Christmas, a memorable herbal holiday. In 1987 Mrs. Simmons's book was reintroduced by Rodale Press as *Herbs Through the Seasons* and is now available in enlarged format complete with many new photographs and a full-color cover.

Herbs and the Earth by Henry Beston (circa 1935) is my favorite of favorites. It's not just a how-to book as his prose is poetry and I thrill to every paragraph. When Mr. Beston writes, "A garden of herbs need be no larger than the shadow of a bush, yet within it, as in no other, a mood of the earth approaches and encounters the spirit of man," I find myself nodding in agreement then rereading his well-turned phrases. First acquired as a paperback reprint, this slim volume joined me at breakfast for years, my start-of-the-day companion. So enamored am I of *Herbs and the Earth,* I sought out a hard-cover edition from a rare book dealer, well worth any price. Now I have a copy upstairs and another downstairs. This extraordinary literary herbal has now been reprinted by The Herb Society of America and is available through them (for address, *see* page 169).

Helen Noyes Webster's *Herbs: How to Grow Them and How to Use Them* (circa 1939) is a gold mine of herbal information to explore. Do you know about herbal snuffs? Along with thirteen alliums and twenty-six artemisias, she lists basils I am still seeking. Many illustrations of both classic and cottage gardens, a concise section on "Fragrant and Bitter Herbs of the Bible" along with a six-page bibliography that has me drooling (I want them all!) are only a small part of this useful book. I was delighted to acquire a copy.

For home remedies and medicinal lore, I turn to *The Herbalist* by Clarence Meyer (published by Indiana Botanic Gardens, Hammond, Indiana). I paid $2.95 in 1965 for my well-worn copy printed in 1918. Still in print, it is now $10.95. Another small herbal with equally small print, it packs a walloping amount of information between its five- by seven-inch covers. In the second half, my favorite part, he covers natural dyes, Indian herbs, herbal insecticides, and a nicotine-free herbal tobacco that surely would cure one of smoking. Cosmetics, weight control, gargles, botanical vinegars for every purpose, chewing gums, much on fragrant sachets and incense, seasonings to prevent rancidity (antioxidants) are among the amazing disclosures. Even the magic of botanical curios is revealed. I get lost browsing through this one.

Finally, the *Golden Guide to Herbs and Spices* (by Golden Press, published by Western Publishing Co., Inc. in Racine, Wisconsin) is so tiny I have several copies, one I carry with me everywhere. Despite its size, it has over 800 listings in its index, lovely colorful pictures for identification, and has rarely failed to answer the obscure questions I so frequently encounter.

There are more, of course, hundreds more in a bewildering array. And I will list a few more I feel are indispensable. But I am addicted to my old herbals, rereading them every chance I get — while resting, traveling, in the bathroom, or on my stationary bike. There's always one of these slim books handy for a quick paragraph. Inspiration leaps off the pages in such stolen moments. To this day I discover new things — or thrill to rediscovery — in my old favorites.

Believe it or not, this basic collection, the keys to the hidden plant mysteries of the universe, takes up a mere five inches on my bookshelf. They are the beloved teachers I owe a great debt for they have taught me a lifestyle. Although no herbal has ever hit a bestseller list and it's equally true that no one book has it all, when I open any one of these small treasures, I feel privileged, as if I am unlocking the magical secrets of the ancients.

There are countless other herbals available and each one has something to offer. In my library of over a thousand titles, I am hard put to determine which to keep and which to give up. Until I must make that decision, I will keep, and want, and use them all. However, this selection are all "keepers." All of my books have taught me something, but these are "The Masters."

Aikman, Lonnelle. *Nature's Healing Arts: From Folk Medicine to Modern Drugs.* Washington, DC: The National Geographic Society, 1977.

Castleman, Michael. *The Healing Herbs.* Emmaus, PA: Rodale Press, 1991.

Duke, James A. *CRC Handbook of Medicinal Herbs.* Boca Raton, FL: CRC Press, Inc., 1985.

Facciola, Stephen. *Cornucopiea: A Source Book of Edible Plants.* Vista, CA: Kampong Publications, 1990.

Foster, Gertrude B., and Rosemary F. Louden. *Park's Success with Herbs.* Greenwood, SC: Geo. W. Park Seed Co., 1980.

Foster, Stephen. *Herbal Bounty: The Gentle Art of Herb Culture.* Layton, UT: Gibbs M. Smith, Inc., Peregrine Smith Book, 1984.

Gerard, John. *The Herball, or Generall Historie of Plants.* London, 1597; NY: Dover, 1975. (An astonishing compendium of over two thousand plants known and used in the sixteenth century, valuable despite its many errors; filled with old botanical drawings and charming quotes you can use.)

Gibbons, Euell. *Stalking the Wild Asparagus.* New York: David McKay Co., Inc., 1962.

Gips, Kathleen M. *The Language of Flowers: A Book of Victorian Floral Sentiments.* Chagrin Fall, OH: Pine Creek Press, 1990.

Grieve, M. *A Modern Herbal: The Medicinal, Culinary, Cosmetic and Economic Properties, Cultivation and Folk-Lore of Herbs, Grasses, Fungi, Shrubs and Trees With All Their Modern Scientific Uses.* 2 Vols. Darien, CT: Hafner Publishing Co., 1931; reprinted by Dover in paperback.

Huson, Paul. *Mastering Herbalism.* NY: Stein & Day, 1974.

Jacobs, Betty E.M., *Growing and Using Herbs Successfully.* North Adams, MA: Storey Publishing, 1981.

King, Eleanor Anthony. *Bible Plants for American Gardens.* NY: Macmillan, 1941. NY: Dover Publications, 1975.

Kowalchik, Claire, and William H. Hylton, eds. *Rodale's Illustrated Encyclopedia of Herbs.* Emmaus, PA: Rodale Press, 1987.

Leighton, Ann. *American Gardens in the Eighteenth Century "For Use or For Delight."* Boston, MA: Houghton Mifflin Co., 1976.

———. *American Gardens of the Nineteenth Century "For Comfort and Affluence.* Amherst, MA: The University of Massachusetts Press, 1987.

———. *Early American Gardens "For Meate or Medicine."* Boston, MA: Houghton Mifflin, 1970.

Lust, John. *The Herb Book.* NY: Benedict Lust Publications, 1974.

Marcin, Marietta Marshall. *Herbal Tea Gardens.* North Adams, MA: Storey Publishing, 1993.

McRae, Bobbi A. *The Herb Companion: Wishbook and Resource Guide.* Loveland, CA: Interweave Press, 1992.

Oster, Maggie. *Herbal Vinegar.* North Adams, MA: Storey Publishing, 1994.

Rose, Jeanne. *Herbs and Things.* NY: Workman Publishing Co., 1972.

Shaudys, Phyllis V. *Herbal Treasures: Inspiring Month-by-Month Projects for Gardening, Cooking, and Crafts.* North Adams, MA: Storey Publishing, 1990.

———. *The Pleasure of Herbs: A Month-by-Month Guide to Growing, Using, and Enjoying Herbs.* North Adams, MA: Storey Publishing, 1986.

Tolley, Emelie, and Chris Mead. *Cooking with Herbs.* NY: Clarkson N. Potter, Inc., 1989.

———. *The Herbal Pantry.* NY: Clarkson N. Potter, 1992.

———. *Gifts From the Herb Garden.* NY: Clarkson N. Potter, 1991.

———. *Herbs: Gardens, Decorations, and Recipes.* NY: Clarkson N. Potter, 1985.

Tull, Deleno. *A Practical Guide to Edible and Useful Plants.* Austin, TX: Texas Monthly Press, 1987.

Weiss, Gaea, and Shandor Weiss. *Growing and Using Healing Herbs.* Emmaus, PA: Rodale Press, 1985.

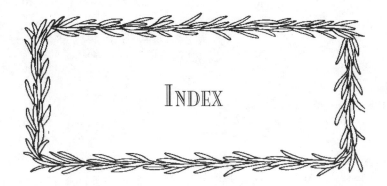

INDEX